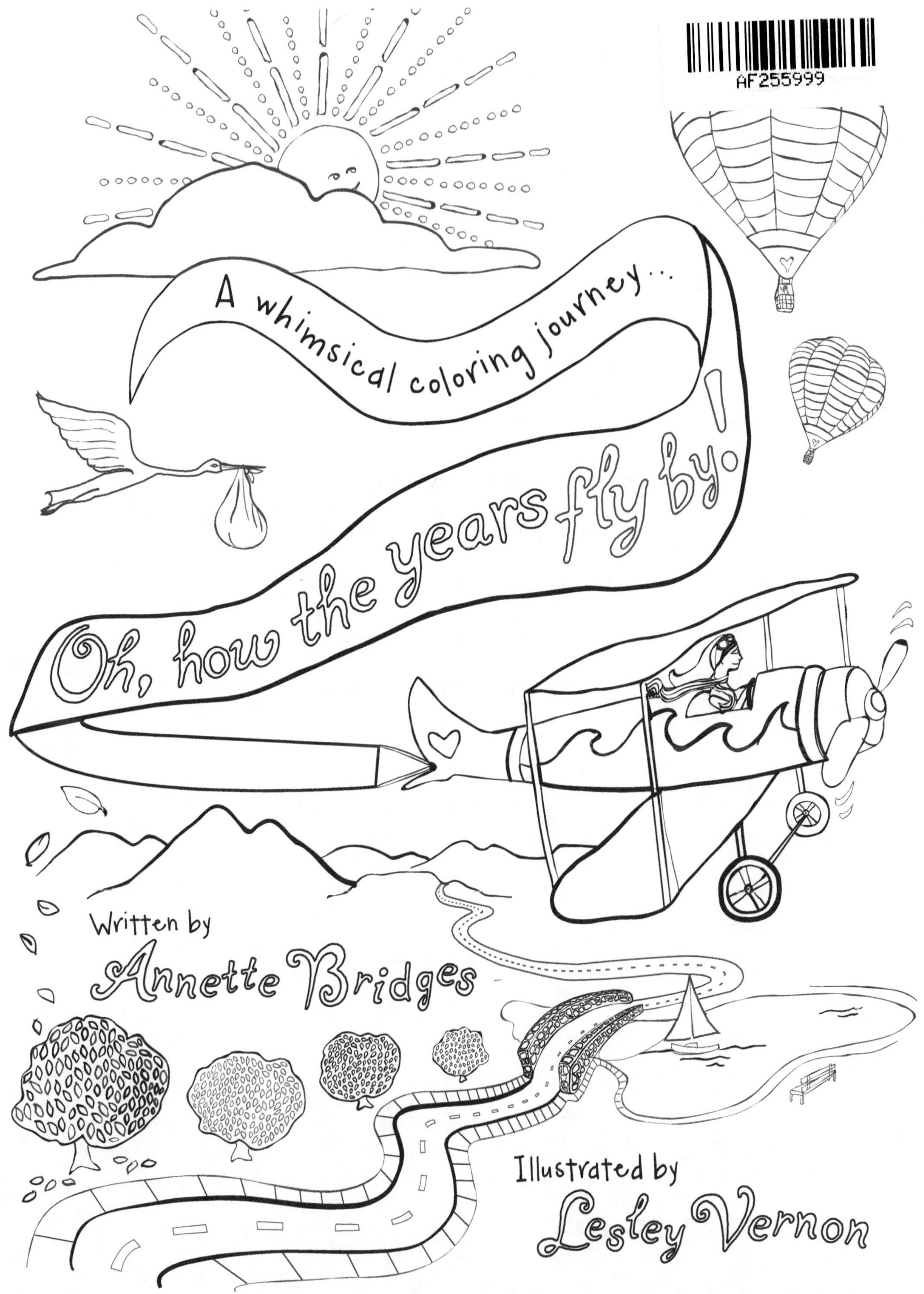

A whimsical coloring journey...
Oh, how the years fly by!
Written by
Annette Bridges
Illustrated by
Lesley Vernon
AF255999

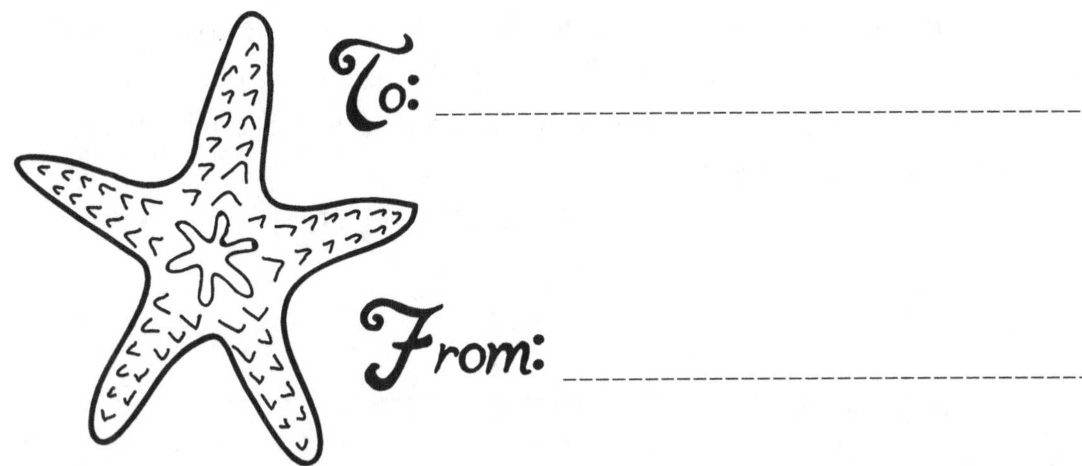
To: _______________________________
From: _______________________________

To my darling daughter Jennifer Bridges,

It was real-life memories captured in your childhood photographs
that inspired every illustration in this book. May we never grow too
old to relive all the fun we had together during your growing up
years; and may these affirmations nourish your soul and refresh your
spirit when you need a boost.

A.B.

To Mason and Ryder,

Witnessing your childhoods is without a doubt the greatest privilege
of my life. Many of the scenes in this book include glimpses of our
own memories so far on our family's journey, and many more are
yet to come. I love you to the moon and back, and will always
treasure our special moments together.

L.V.

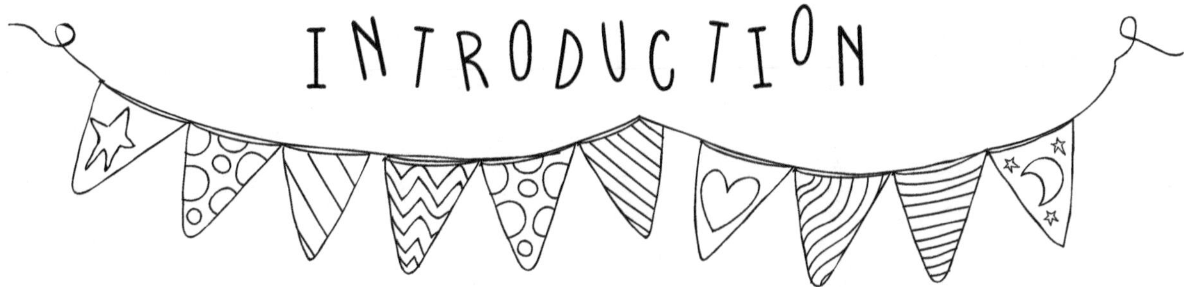

INTRODUCTION

I'm beginning this introduction with a great big Texas "Welcome to my world!" That's because the illustrations so beautifully crafted and designed by my fabulous illustrator Lesley Vernon, began with a stack of photographs depicting adventures with my daughter from her birth to her college graduation.

My hope for you as you color your way through the pages is that you'll be reminded of your own happy childhood exploits and escapades. The years seem to go by so fast. Something I'm feeling more and more as I near my seventh decade.

During times when life feels gloomy or overwhelming and you need a break or a time-out from adult struggles and problems, I hope you'll not only find stress relief in the relaxing art of coloring but joy in being reminded of less complicated days from your own memory bank.

My messages are intended to remind you to keep dreaming new dreams, to assure you that it's never too late to go on new adventures and to encourage you to keep exploring new possibilities and places.

You might be surprised by the pure delight that happens when you get outside and let your gaze look ahead at the horizon before you. Don't forget to look up, too. And take some slow deep breaths.

There are simple pleasures to be enjoyed at every season in our life. And coloring is one of those pleasures. The years may fly by, but there's joy in celebrating memories and in reminding yourself that some moments need to be experienced again and again. Besides, it's never too late and we're never too old to enjoy life's simple pleasures, to play and have fun!

Enjoy!

Love, *Annette*

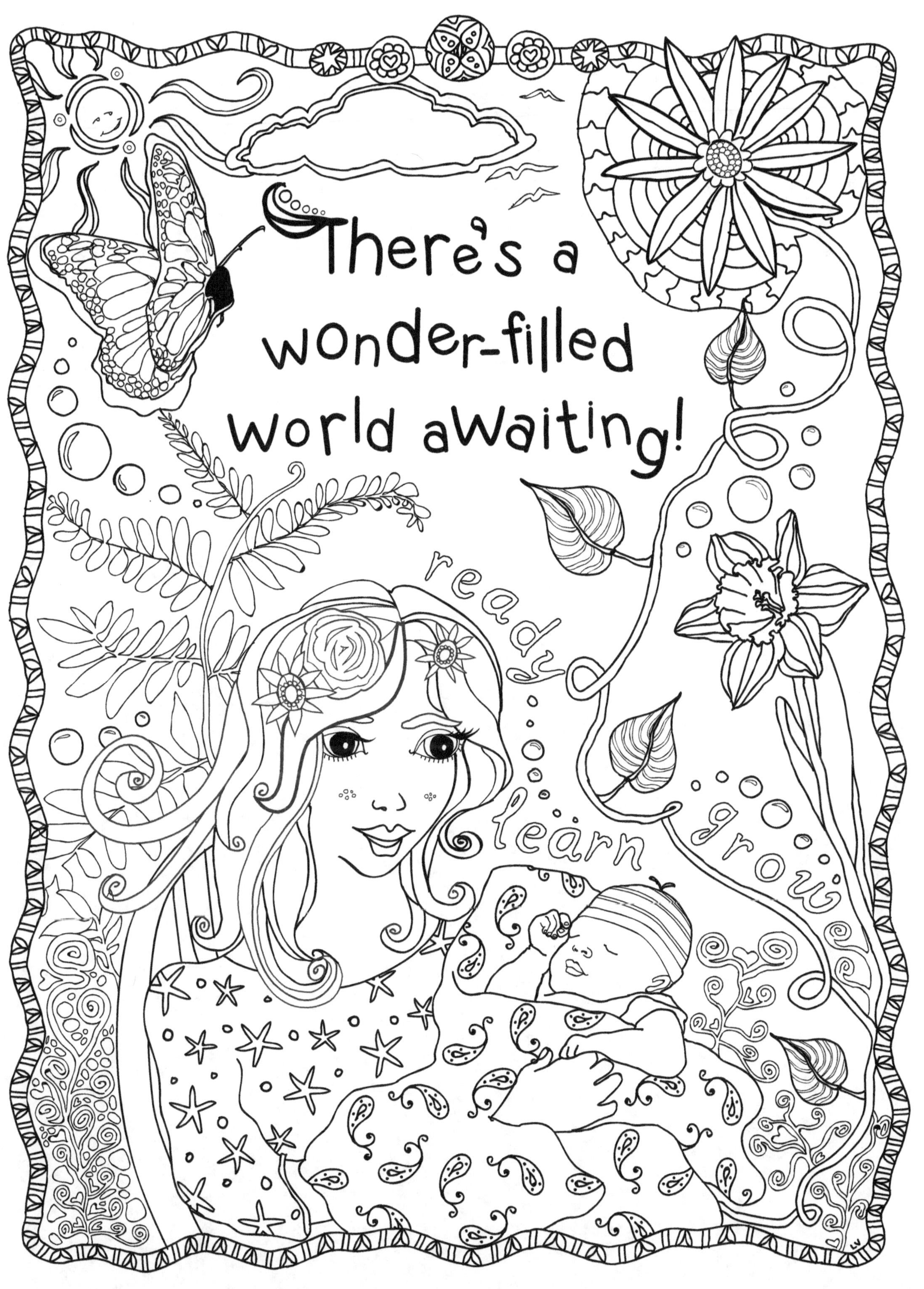

There's a wonder-filled world awaiting!
ready
learn
grow

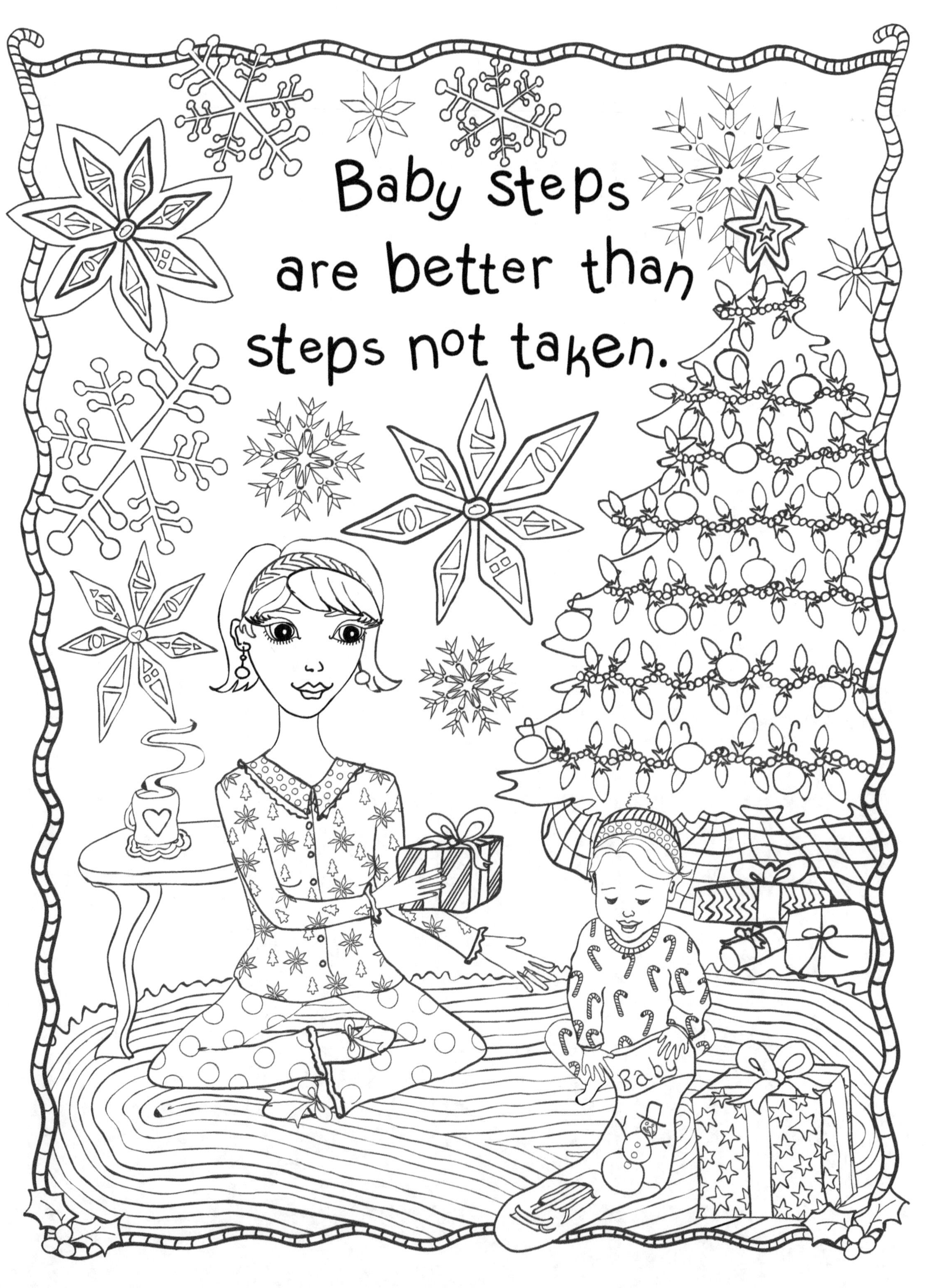

Baby steps
are better than
steps not taken.
Baby

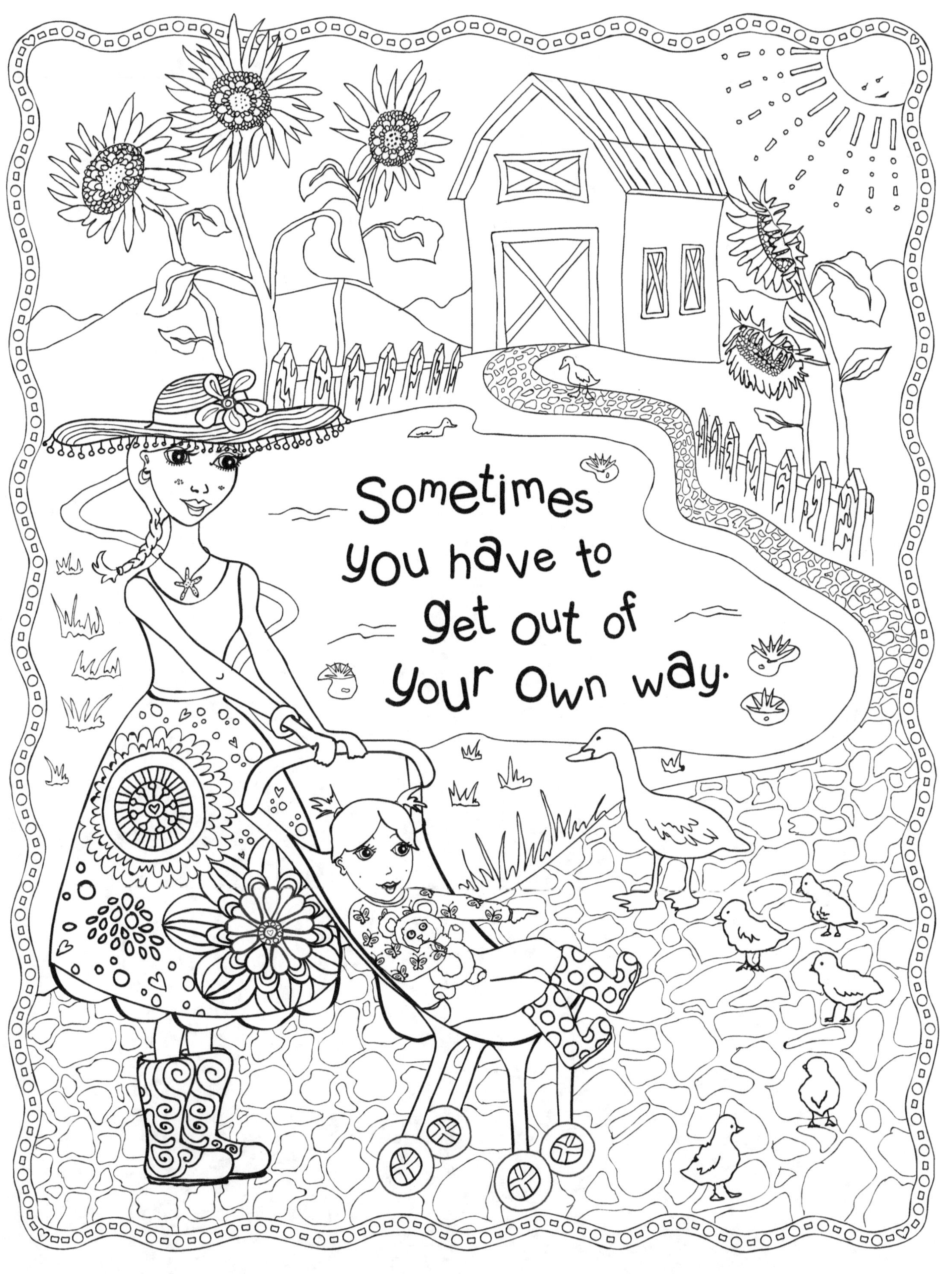

Sometimes
you have to
get out of
your own way.

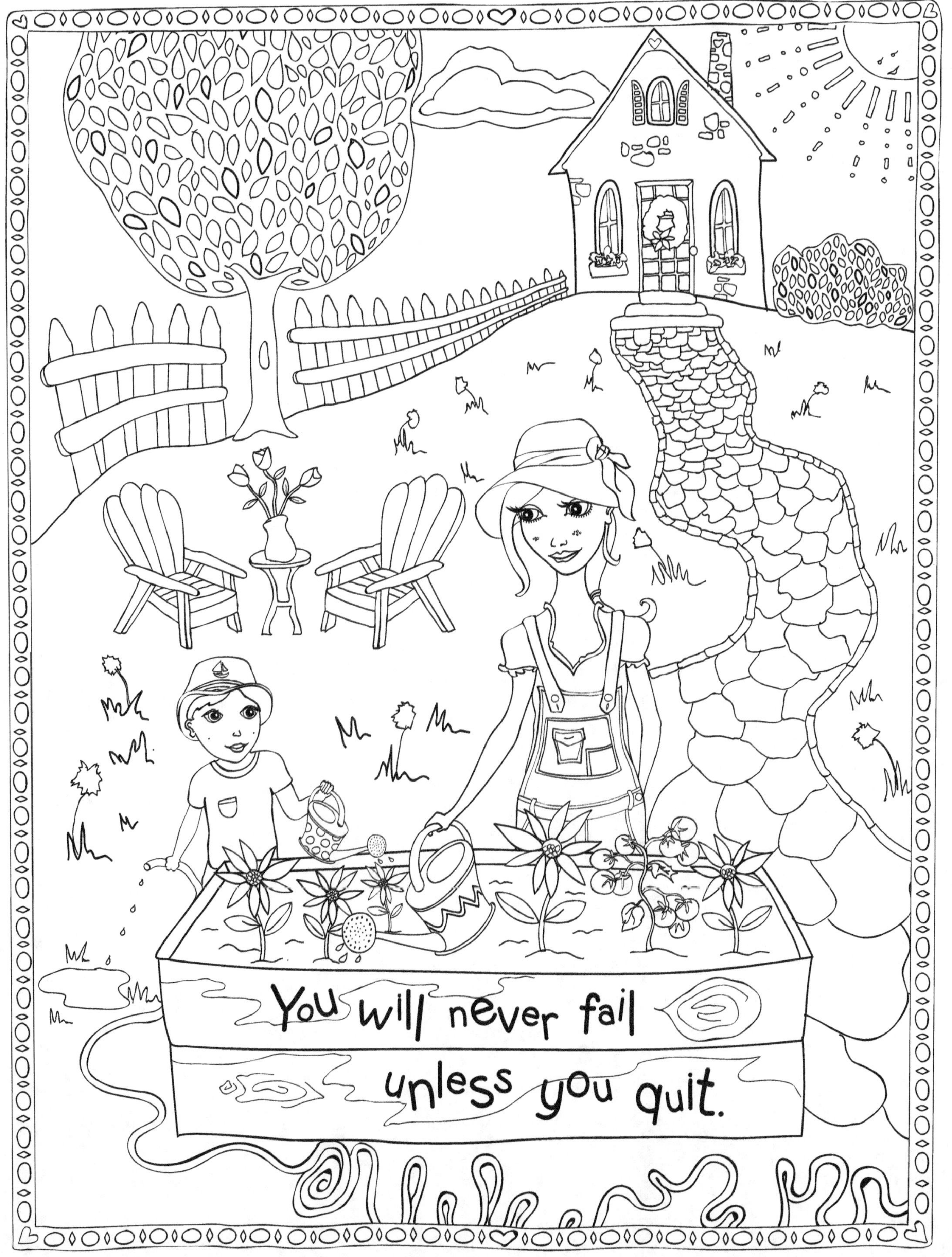
You will never fail
unless you quit.

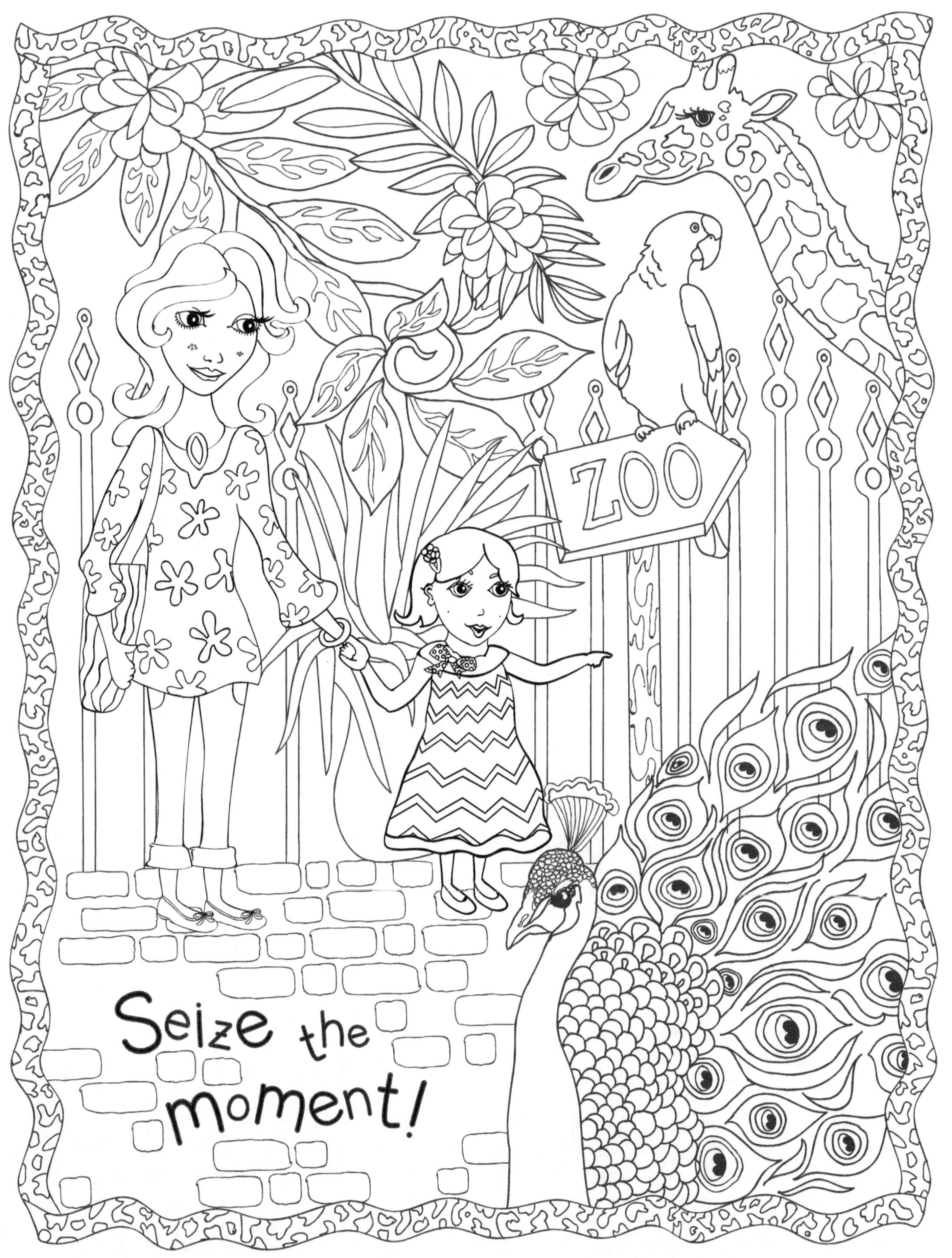

ZOO
Seize the moment!

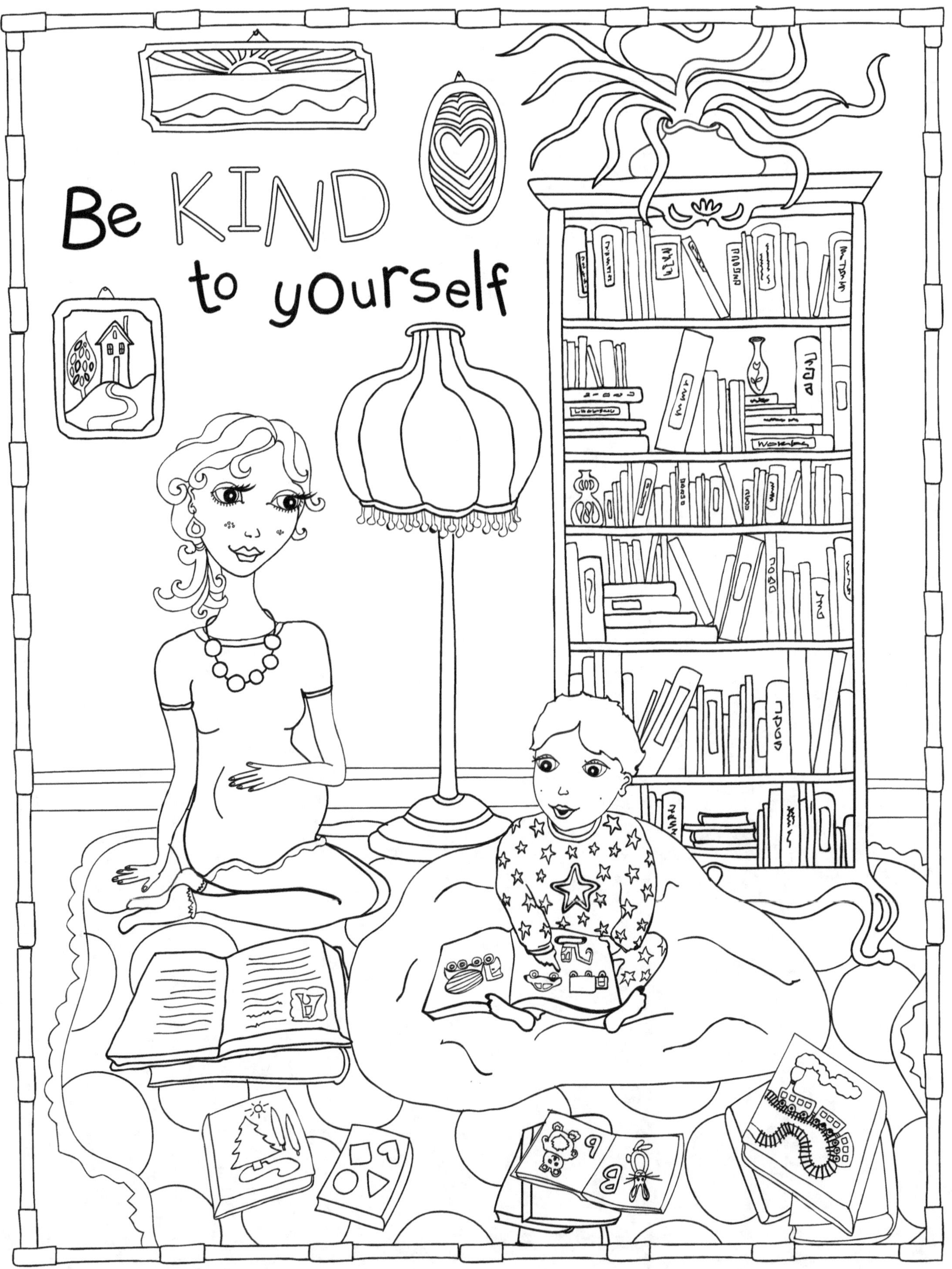
Be KIND
to yourself

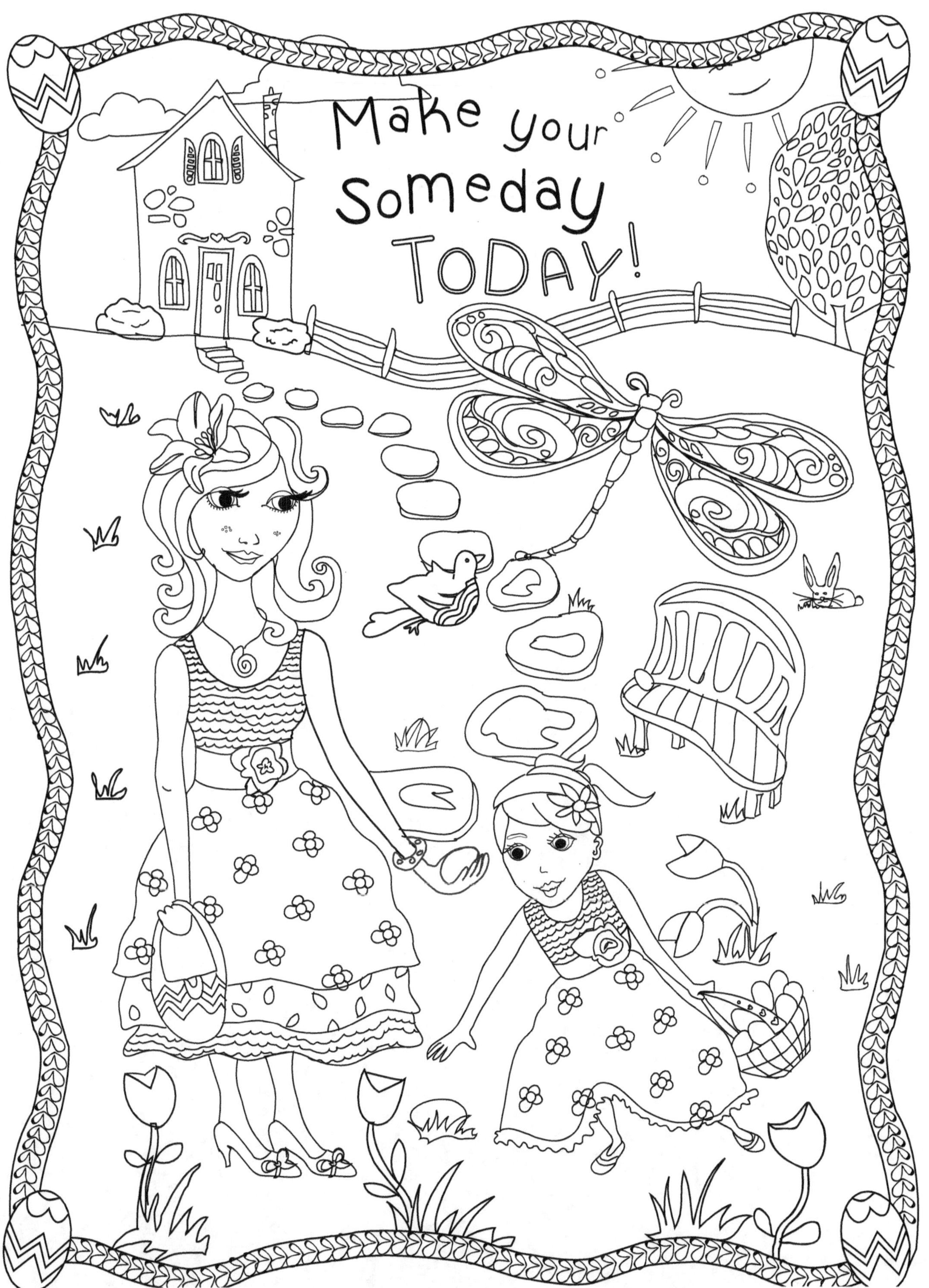

Make your
Someday
TODAY!

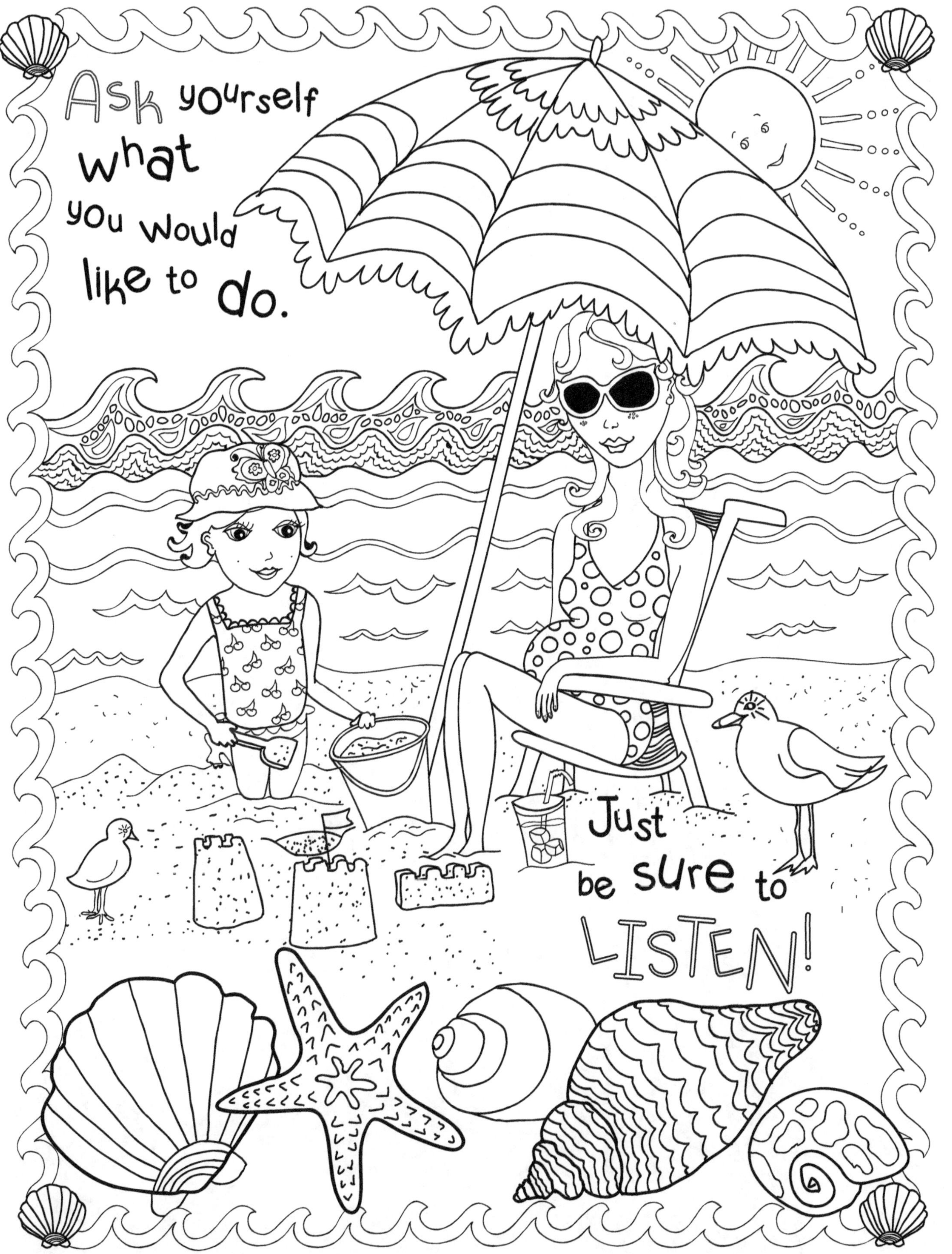

Ask yourself what you would like to do.
Just be sure to LISTEN!

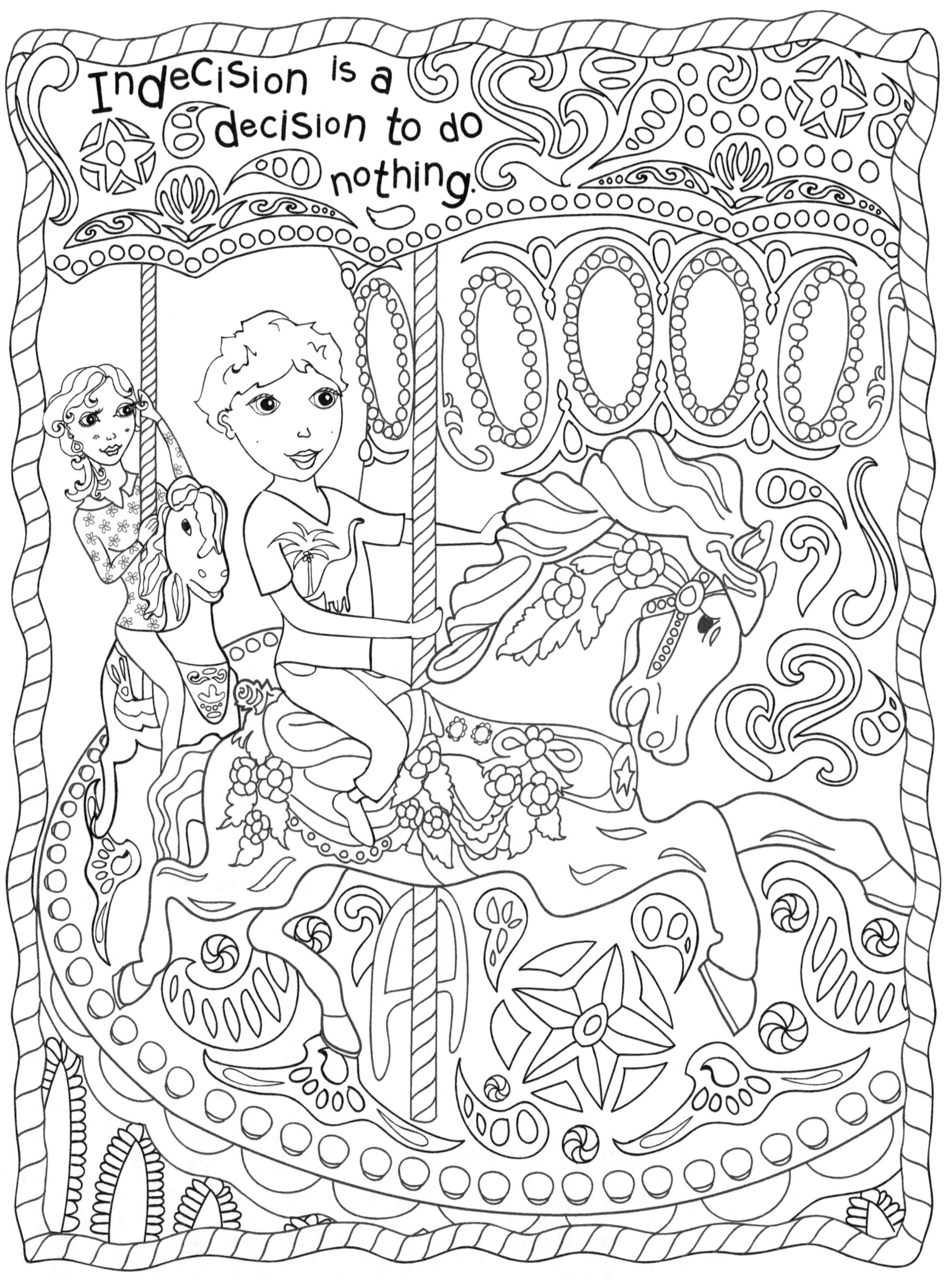

Indecision is a
decision to do
nothing.

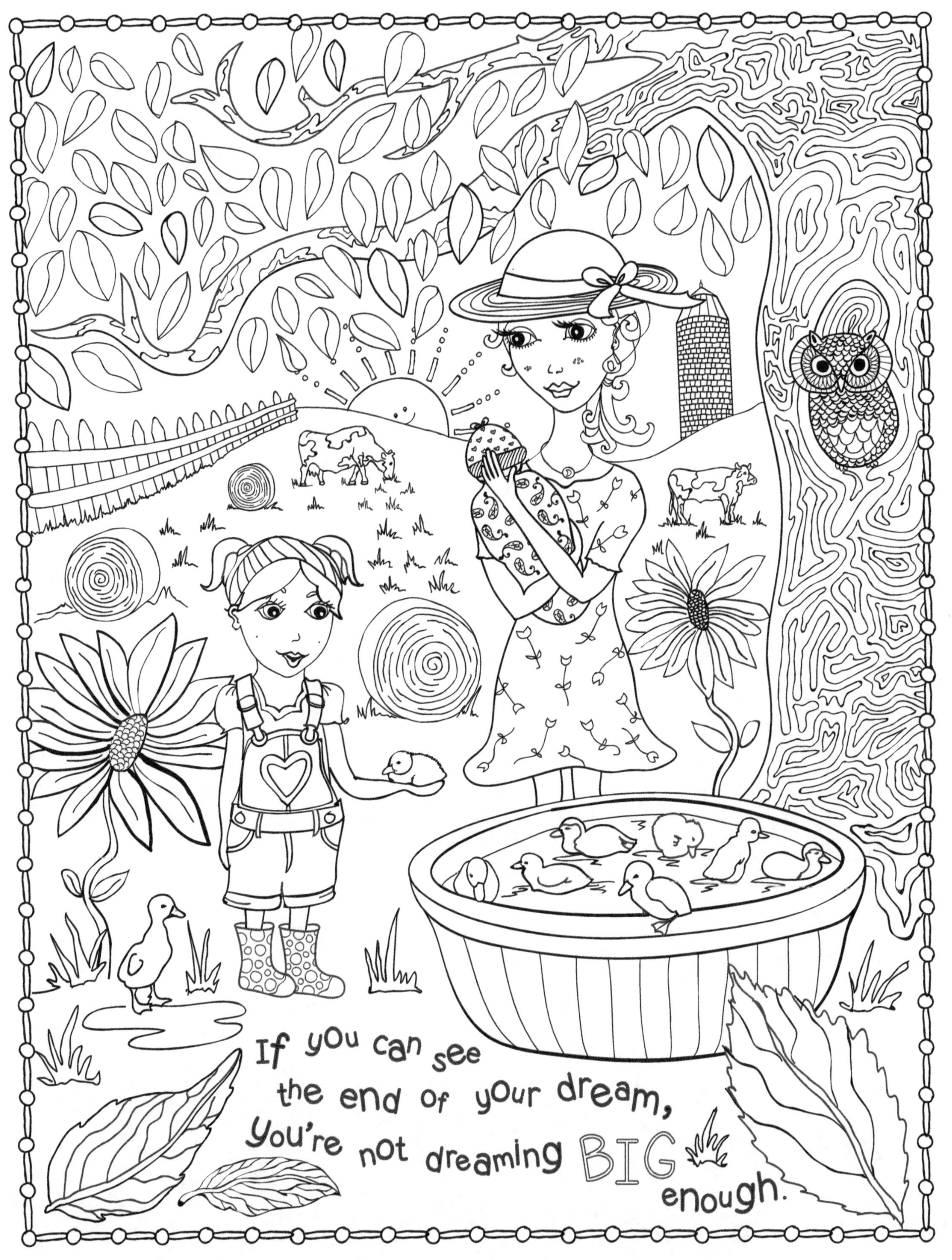

If you can see
the end of your dream,
You're not dreaming BIG
enough.

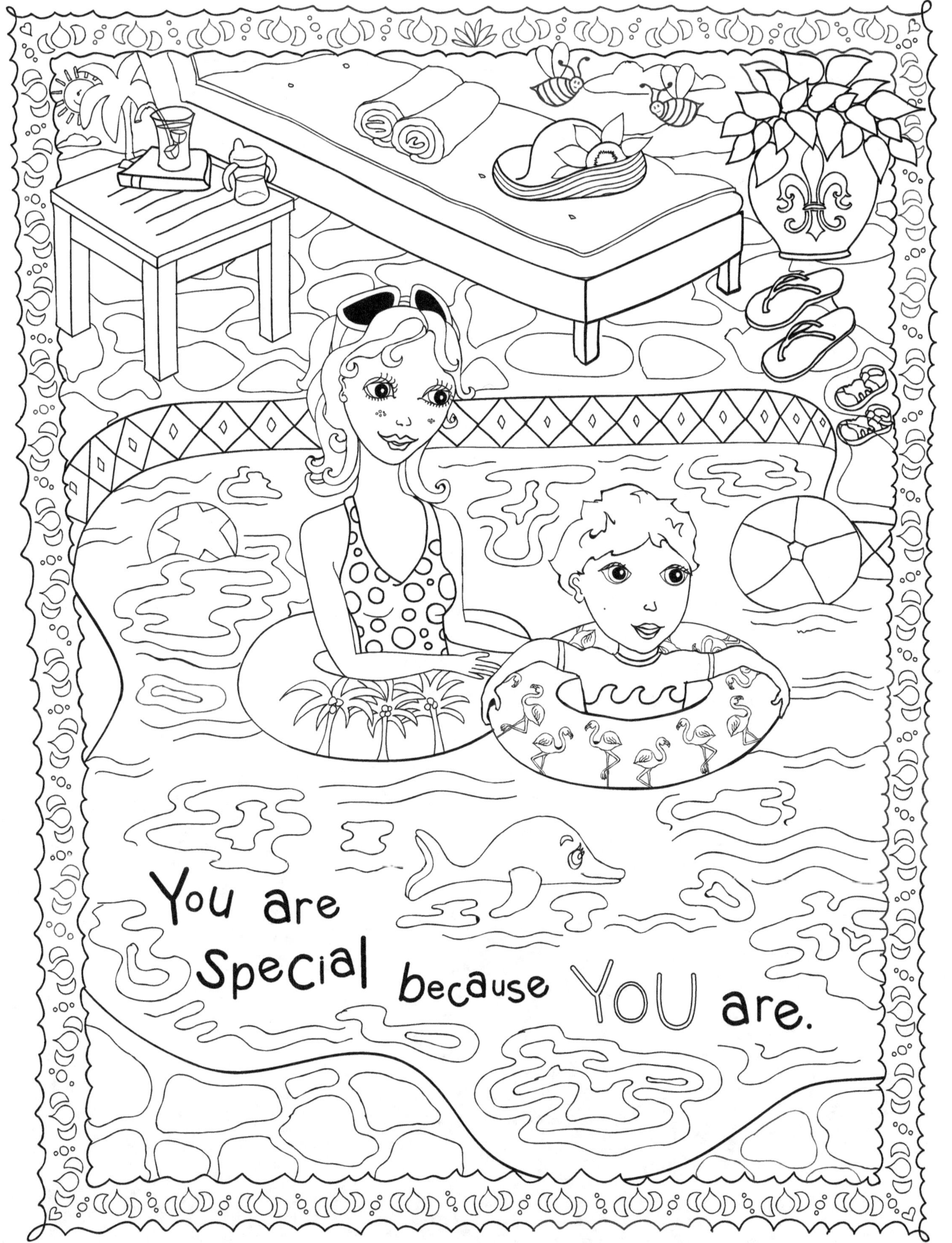

You are
Special because YOU are.

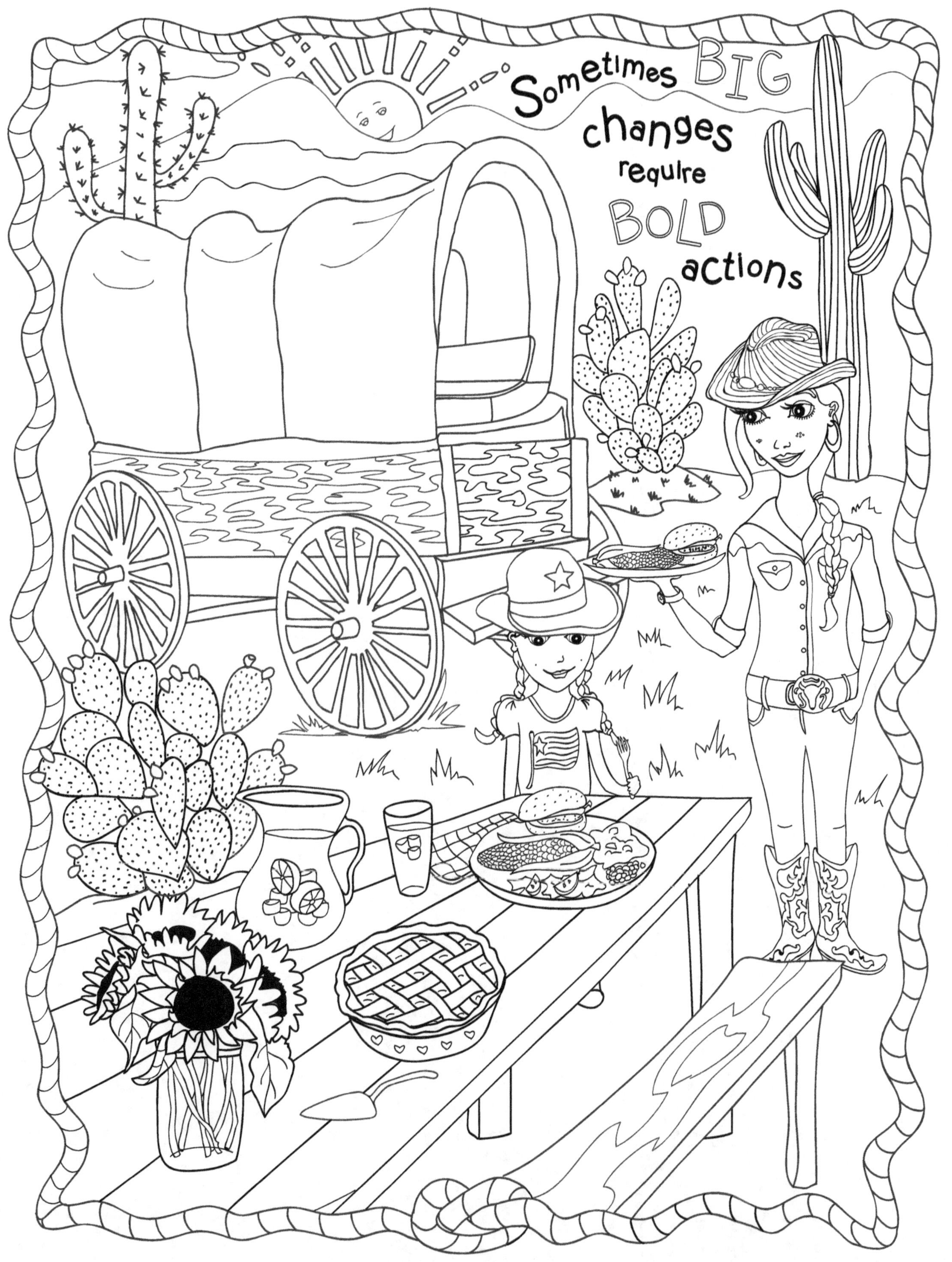

Sometimes BIG
changes
require
BOLD
actions

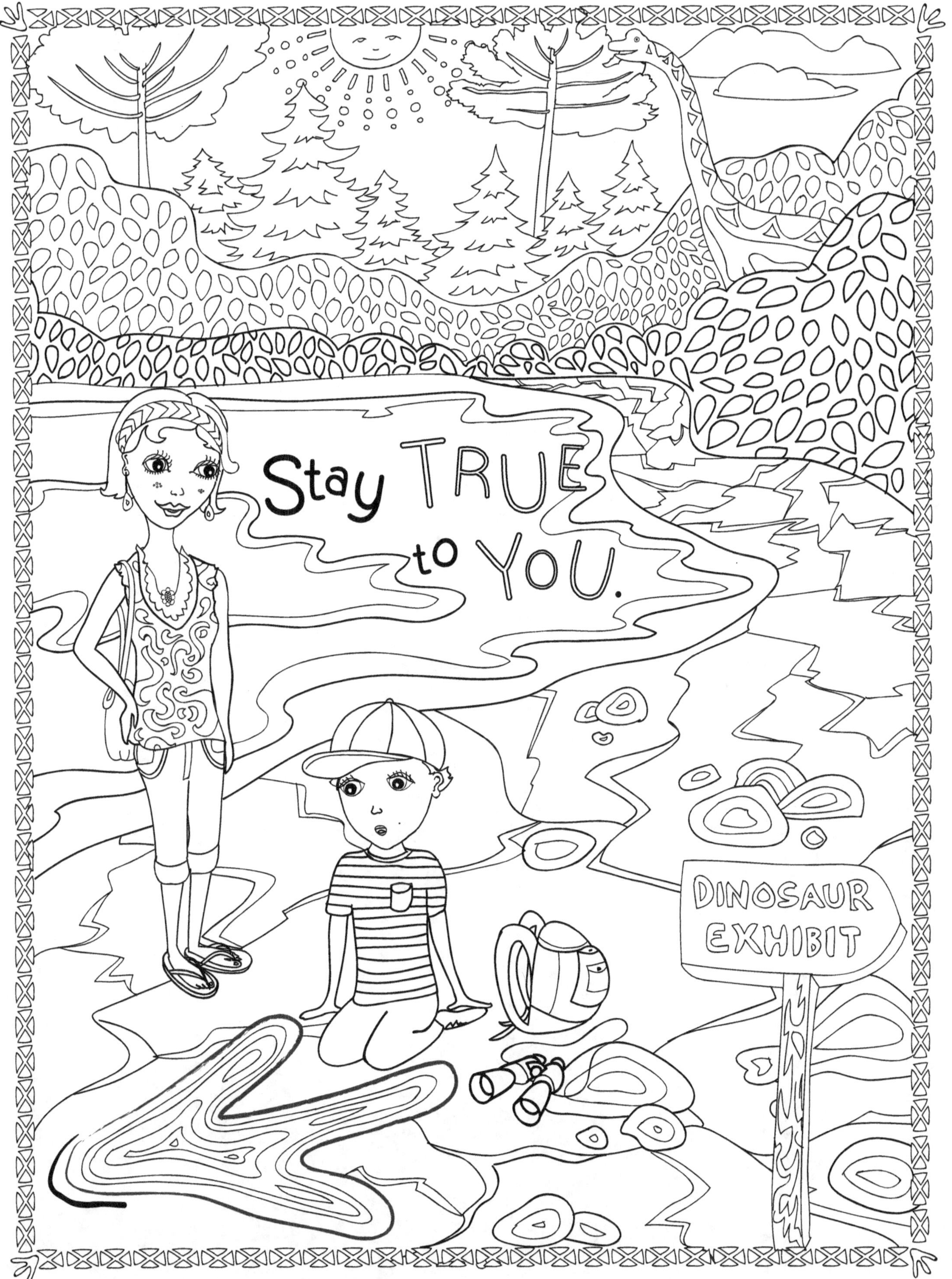

Stay TRUE to YOU.
DINOSAUR EXHIBIT

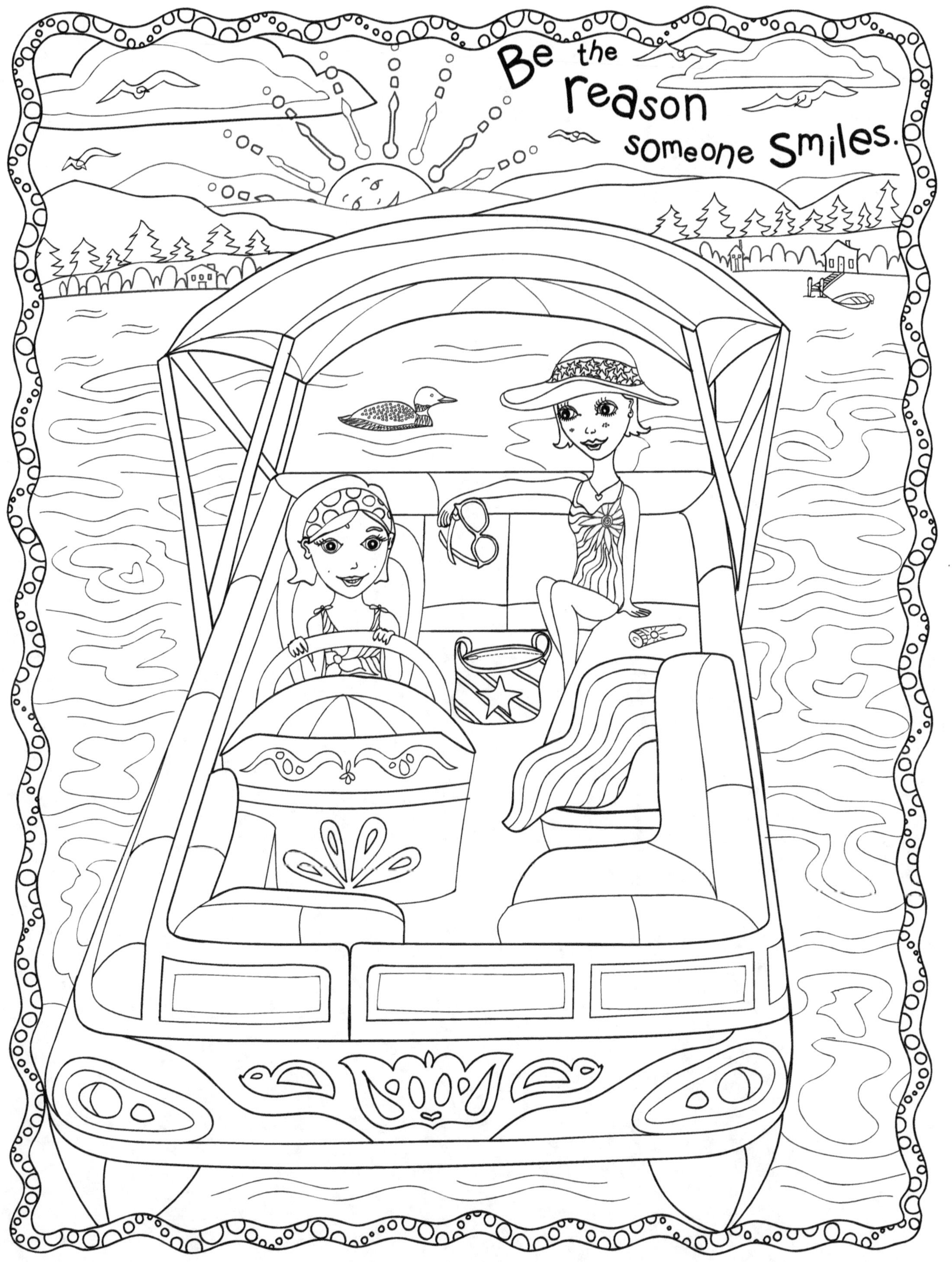

Be the
reason
someone smiles.

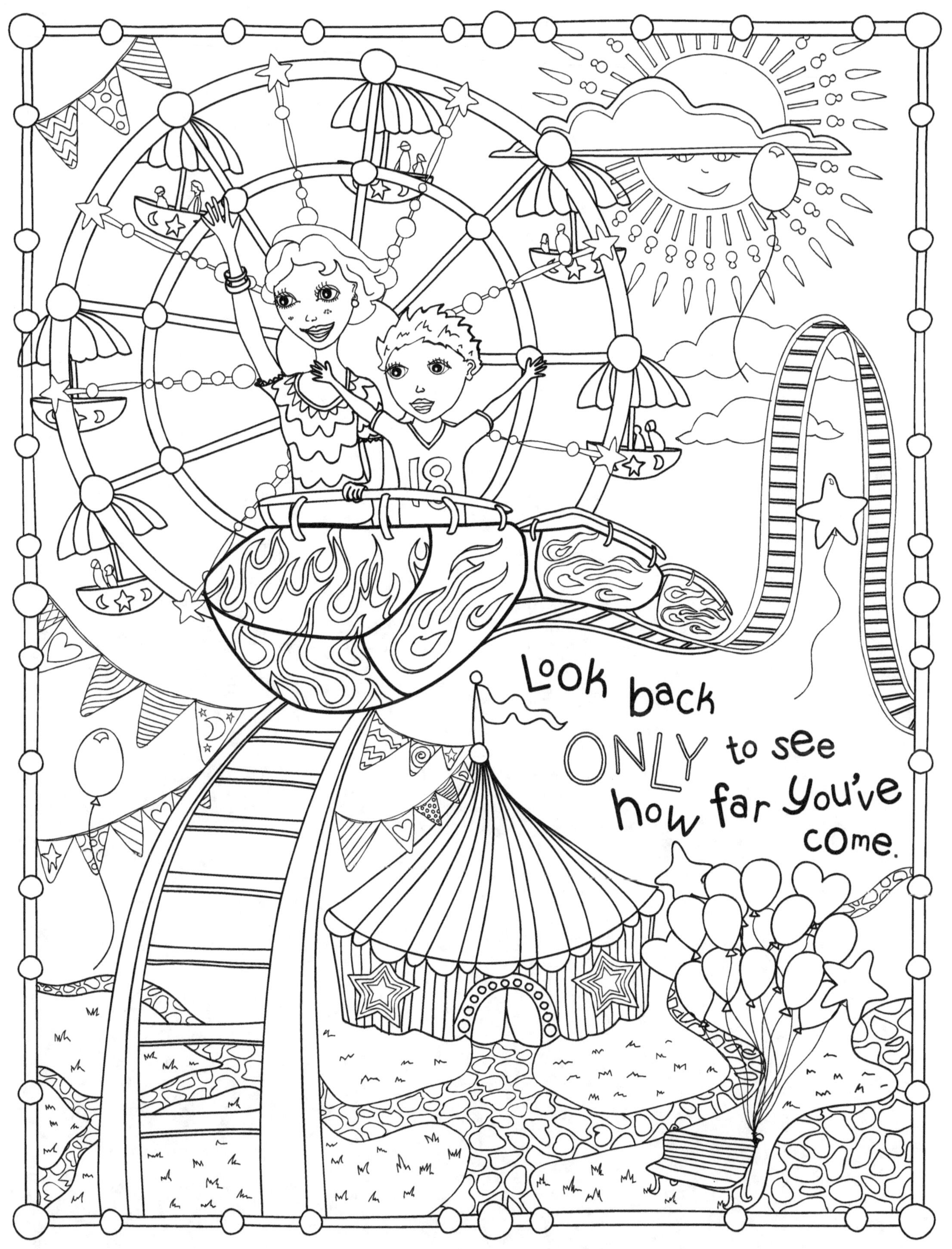

Look back
ONLY to see
how far You've
come.

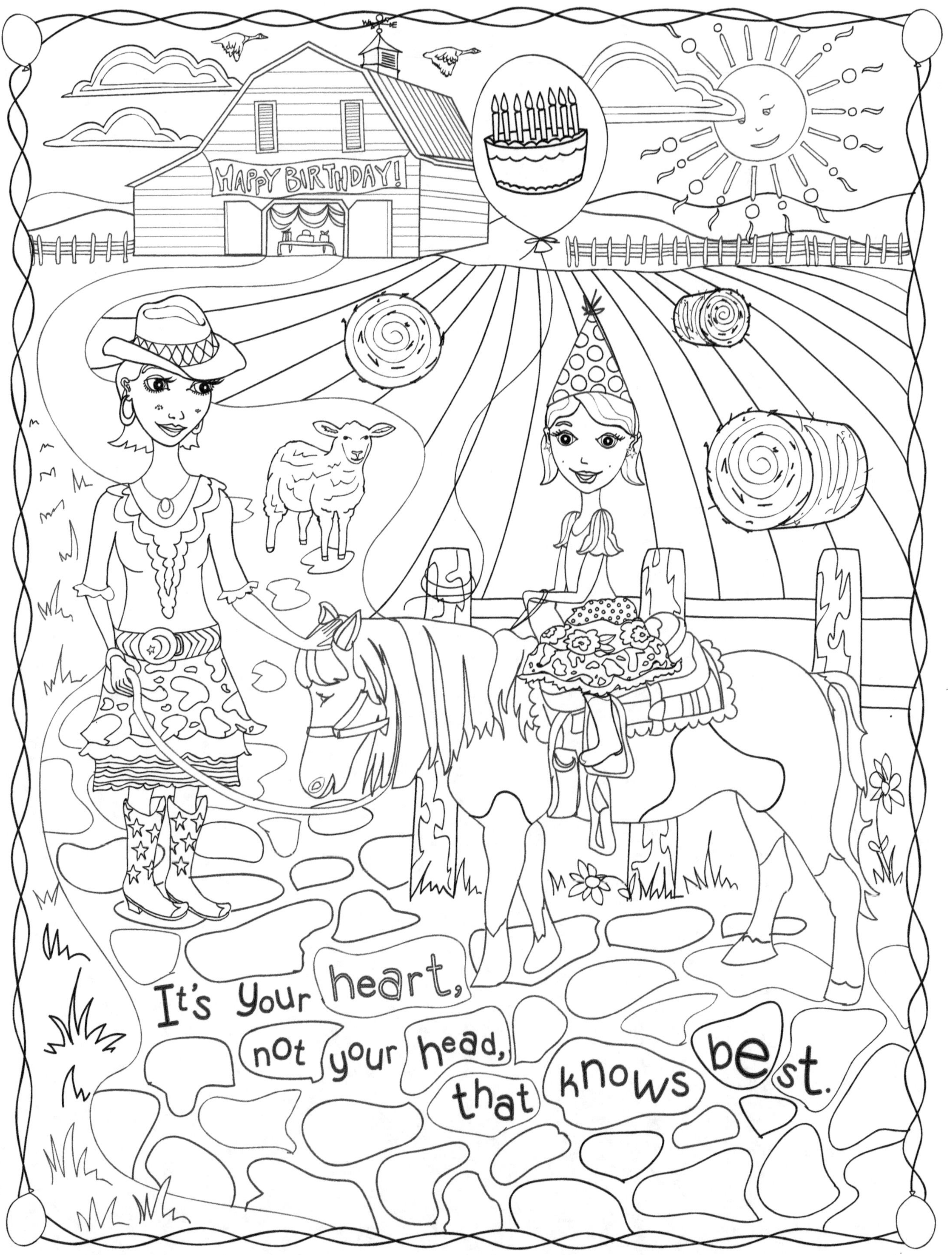

HAPPY BIRTHDAY!
It's your heart, not your head, that knows best.

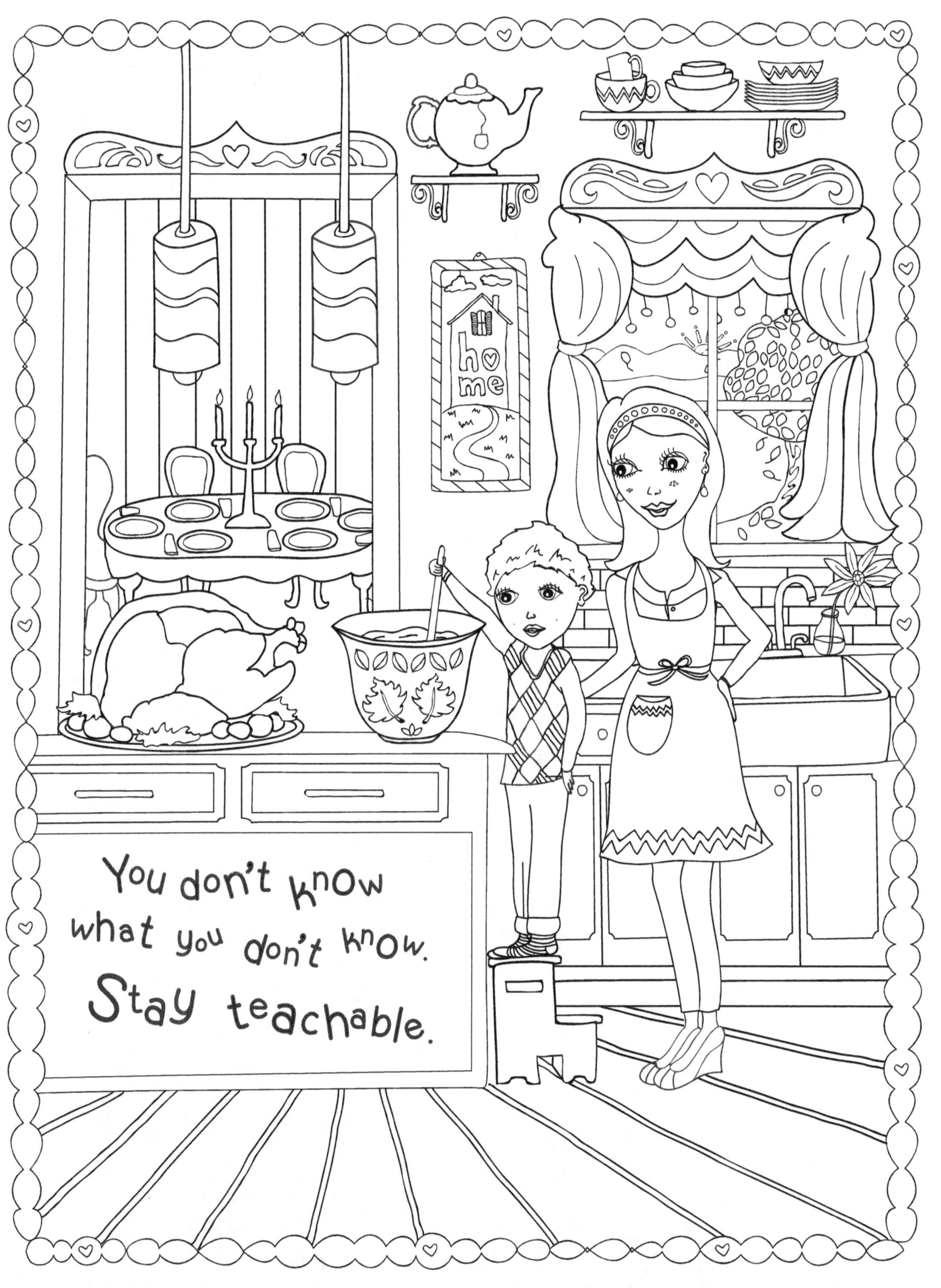
You don't know
what you don't know.
Stay teachable.

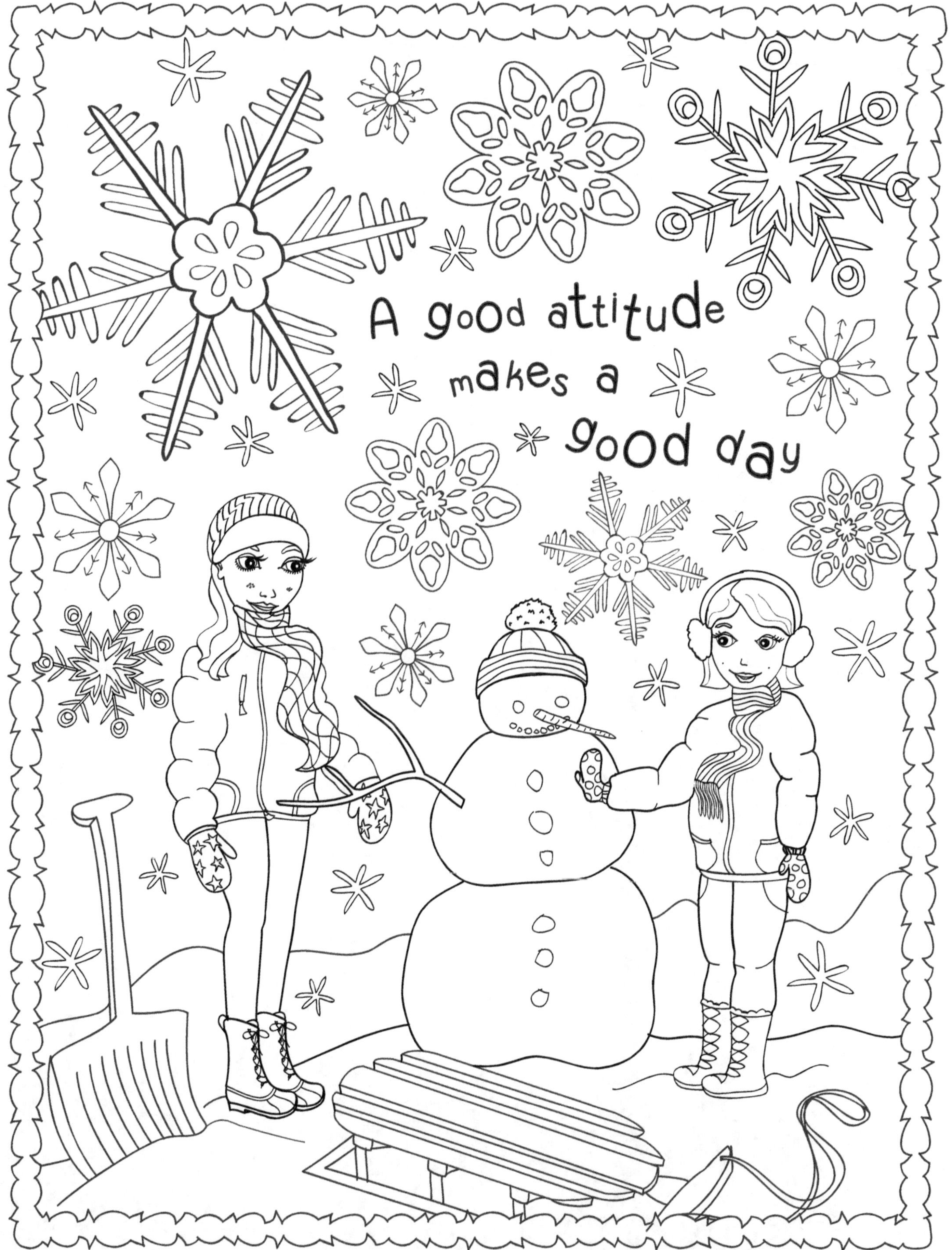

A good attitude
makes a
good day

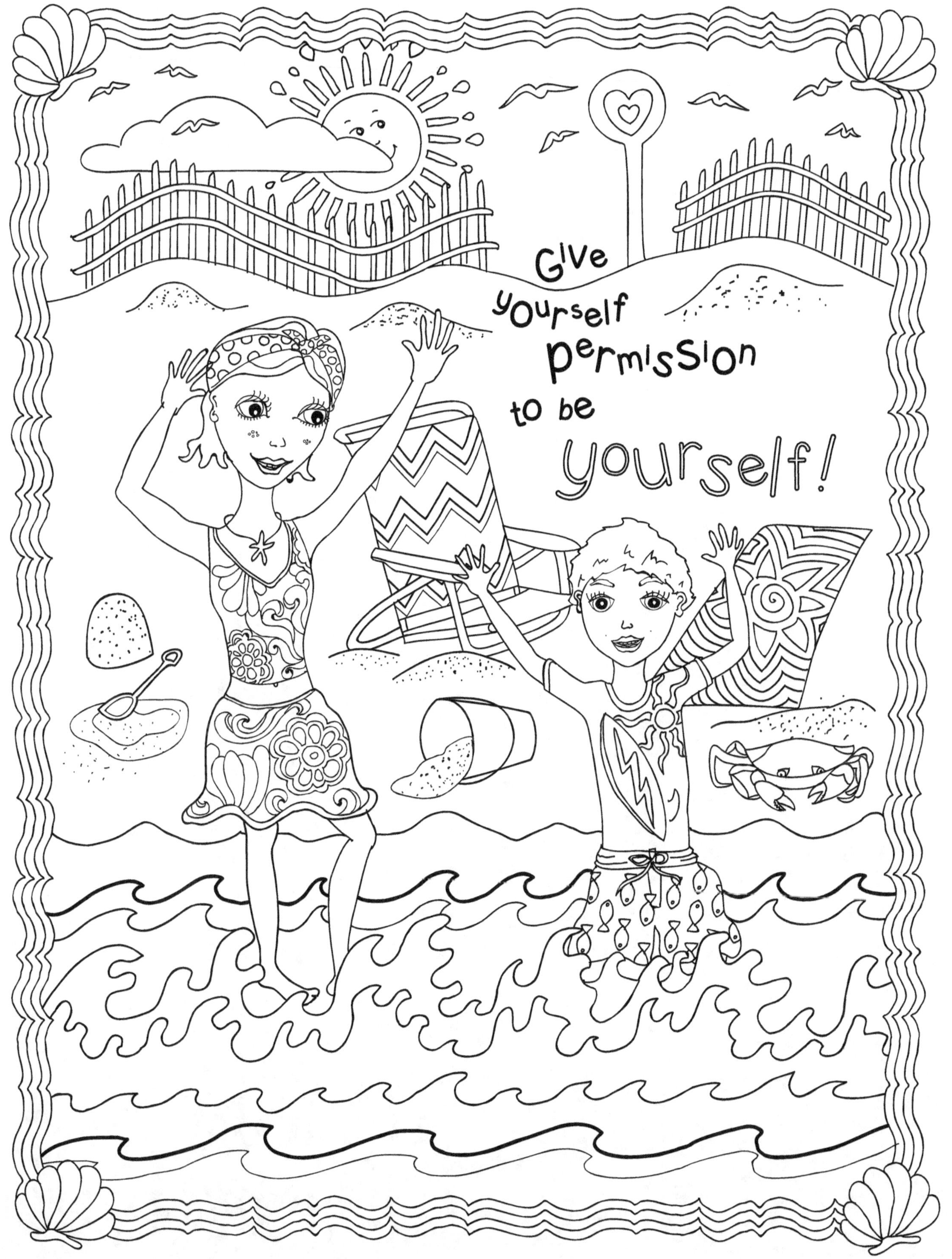

Give
yourself
permission
to be
yourself!

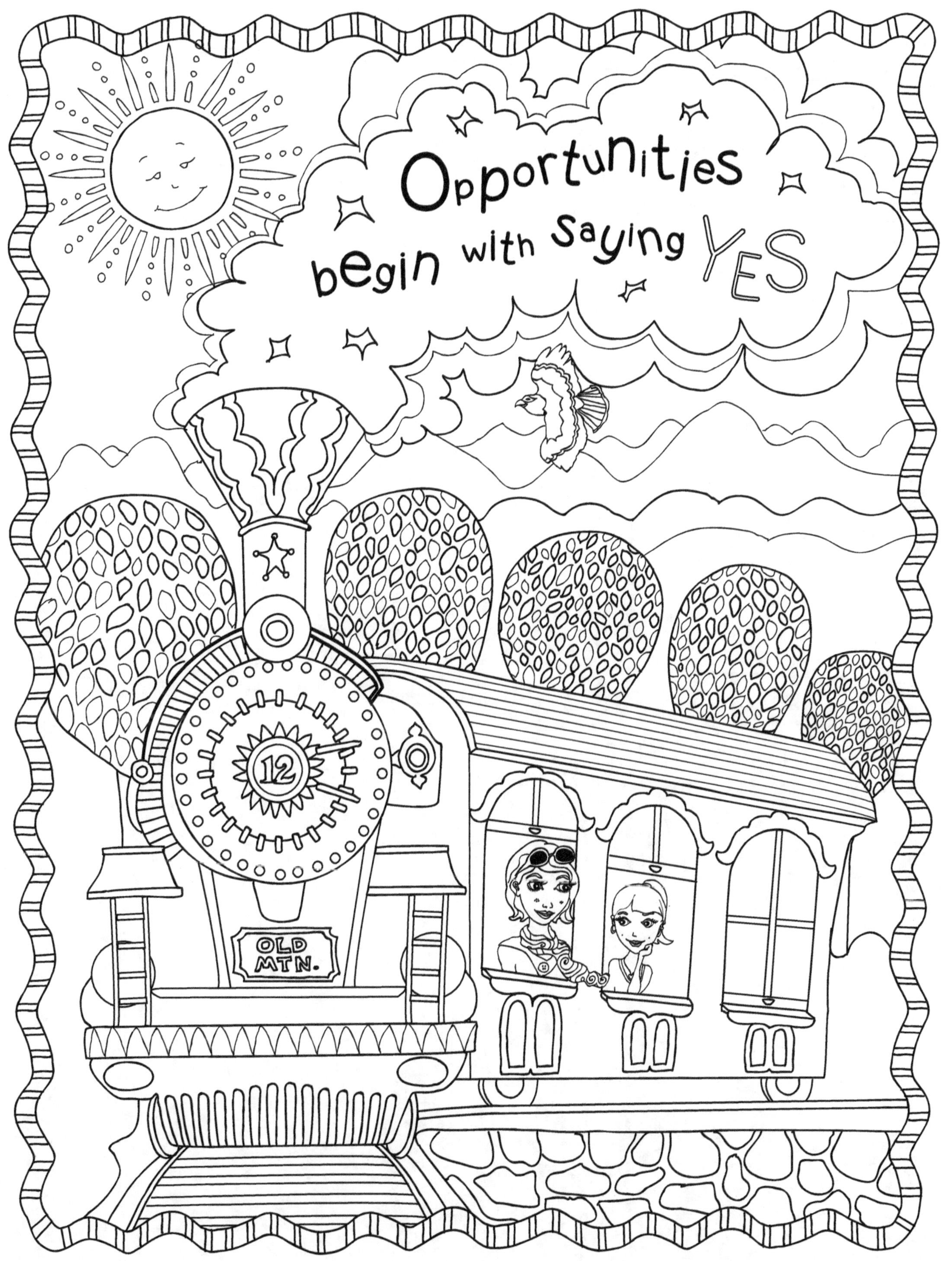

Opportunities begin with saying YES
12
OLD MTN.

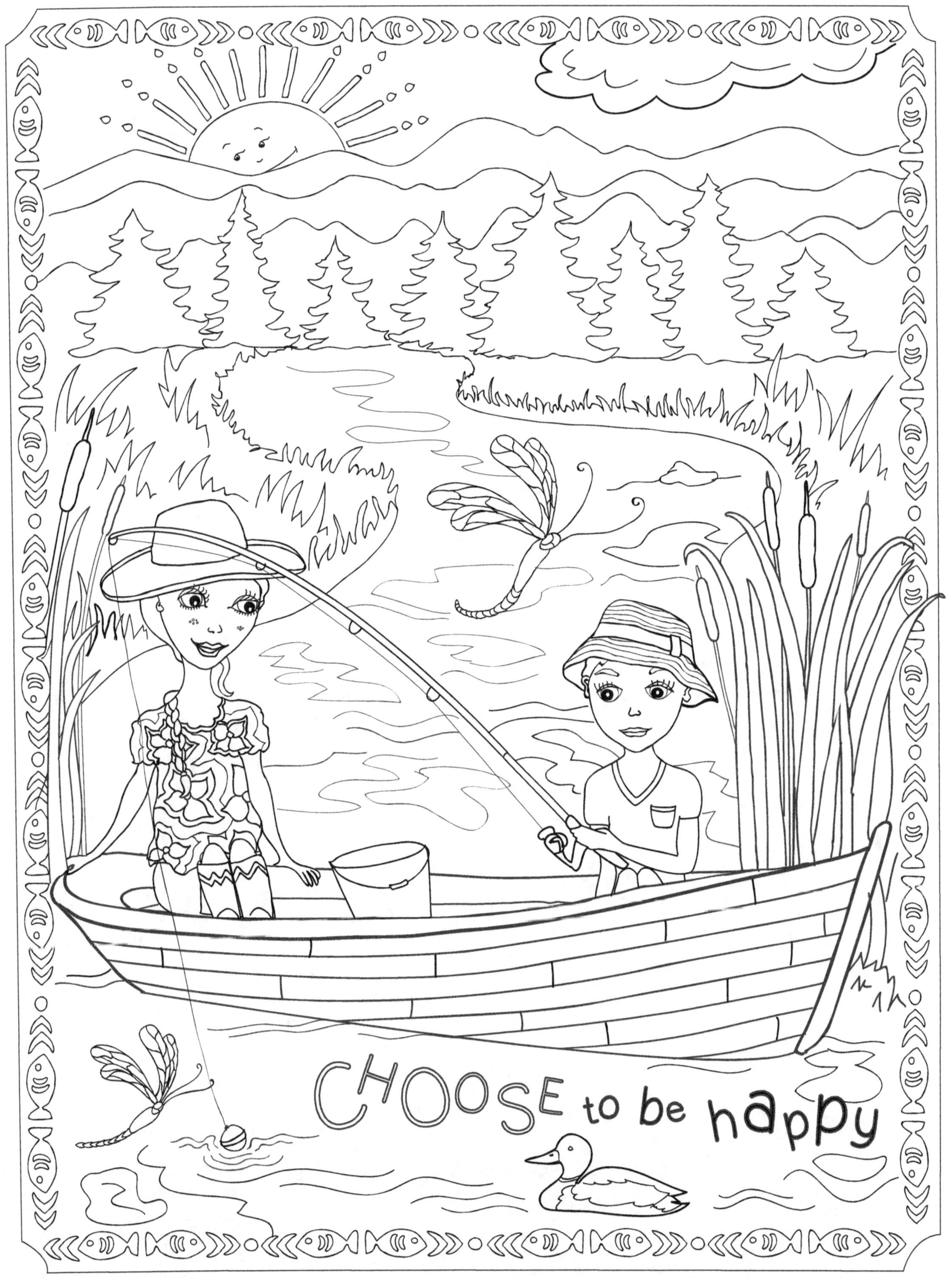

CHOOSE to be happy

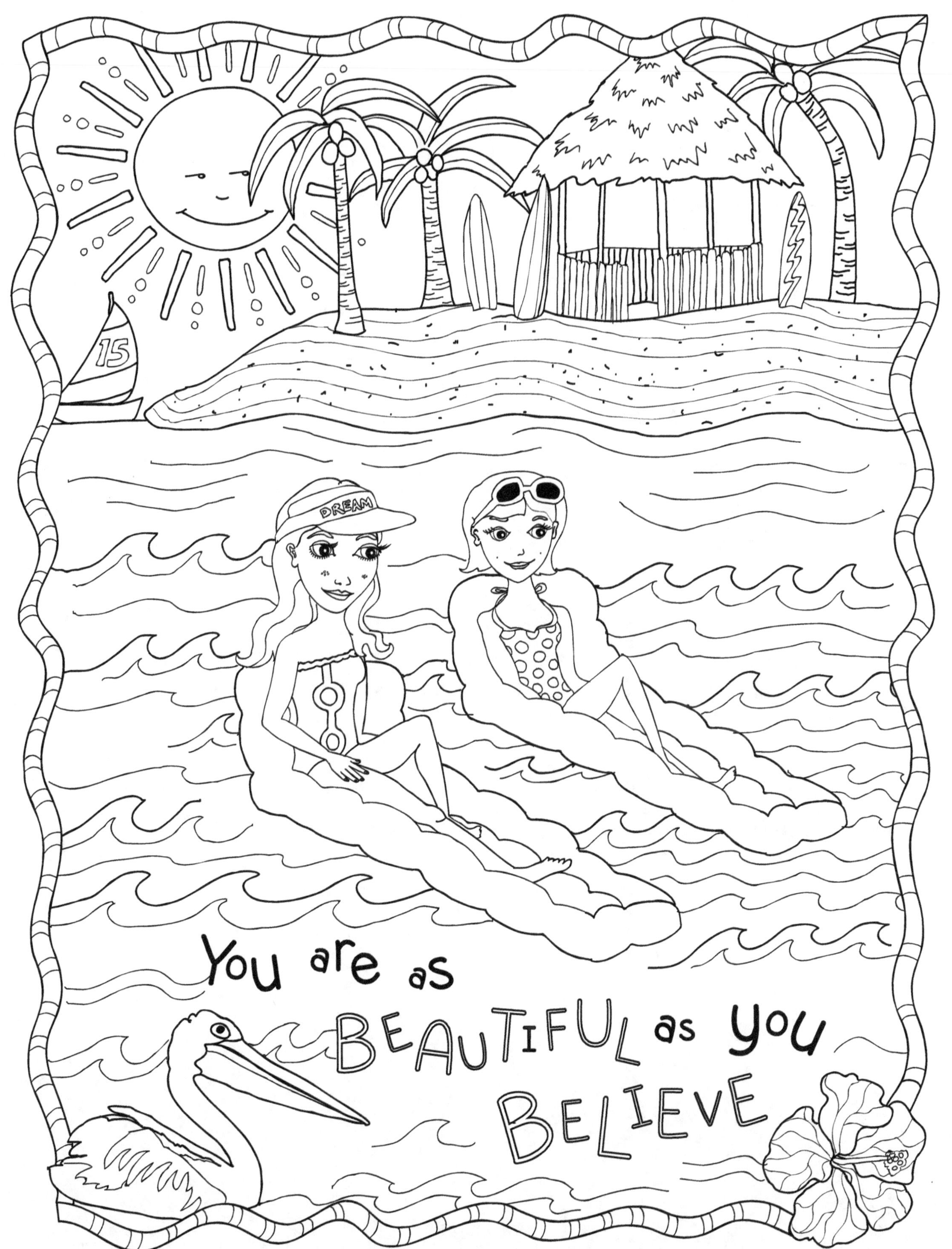

DREAM
15
You are as
BEAUTIFUL as YOU
BELIEVE

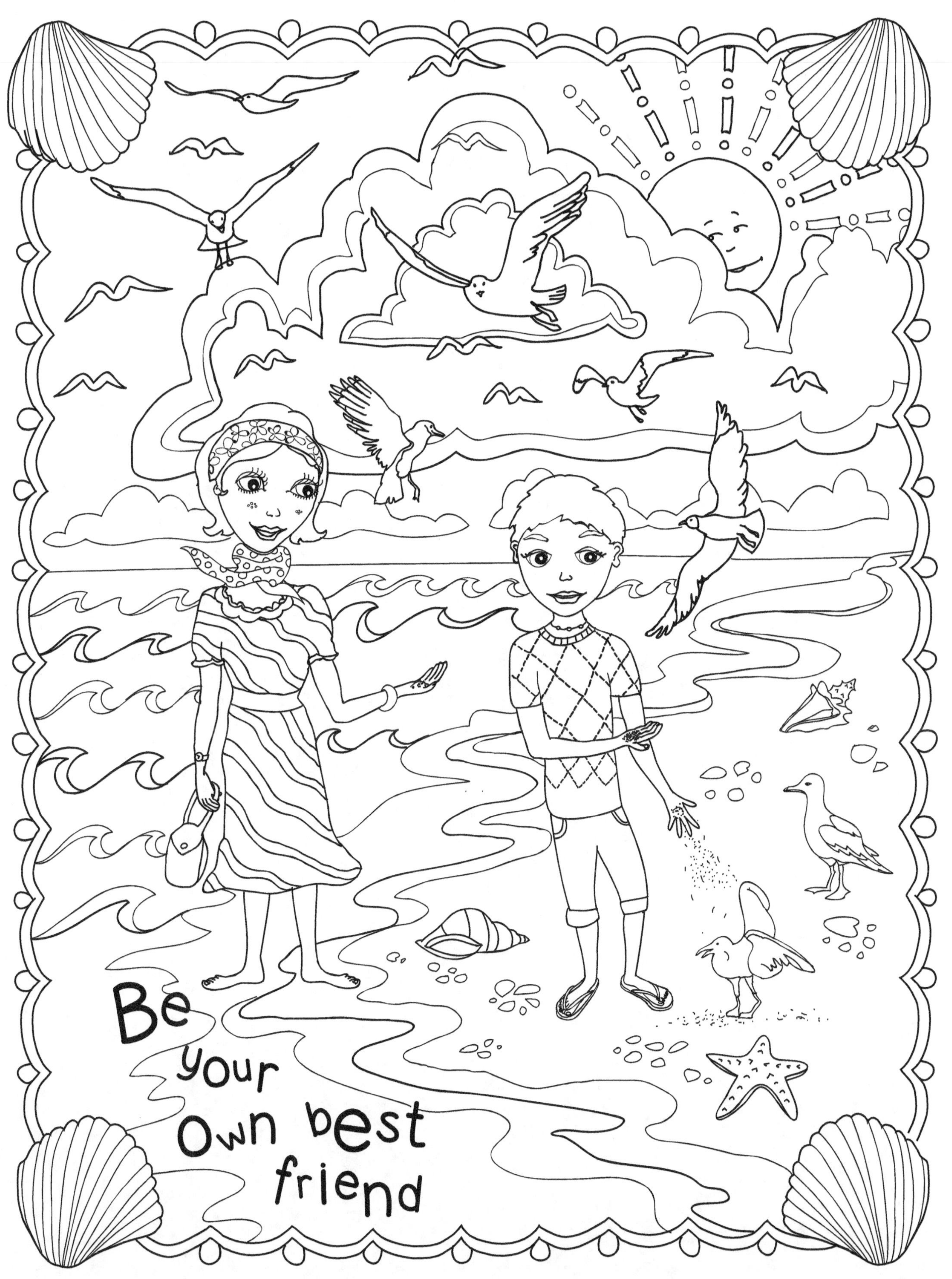

Be
your
own best
friend

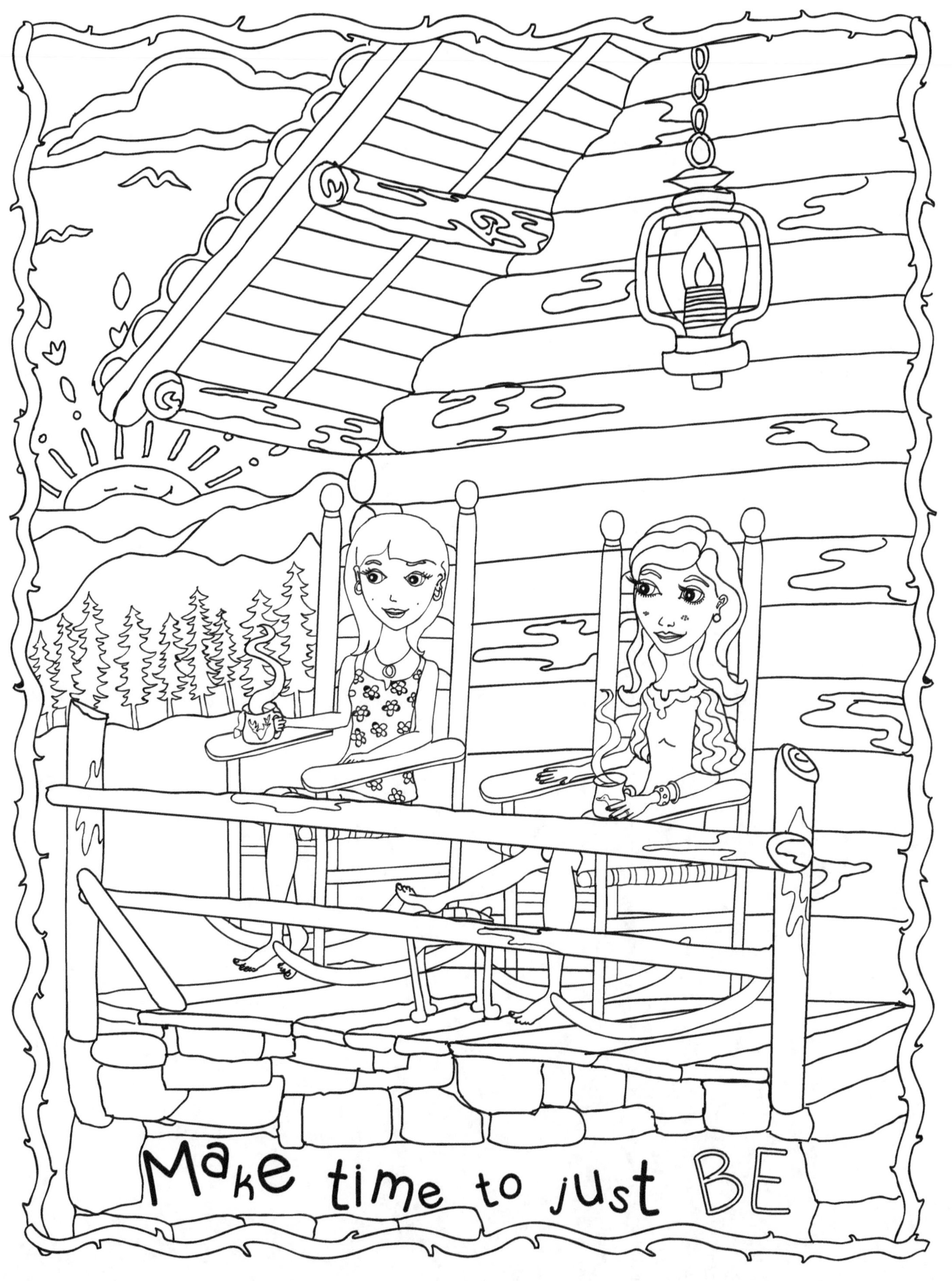

MaKe time to just BE

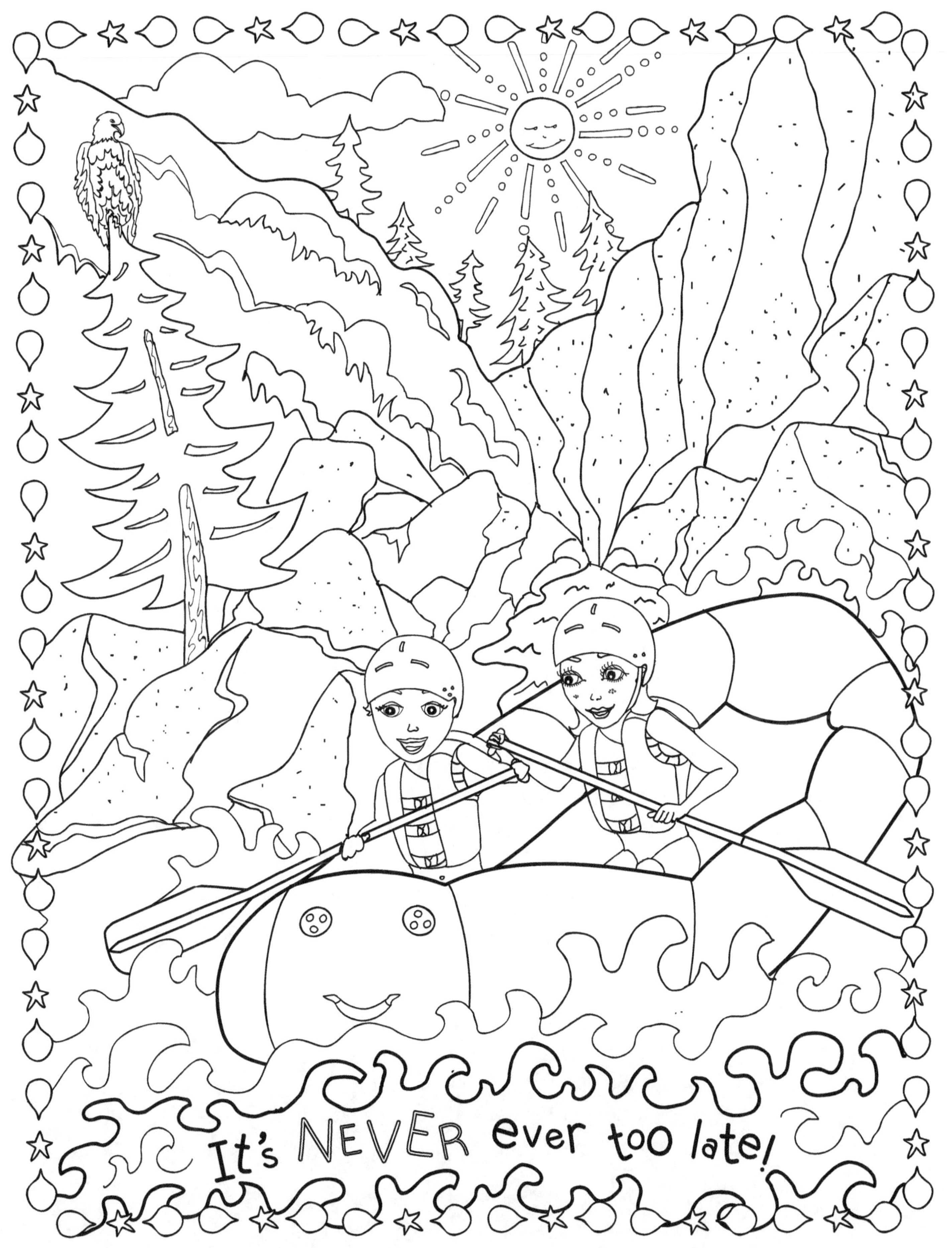

It's NEVER ever too late!

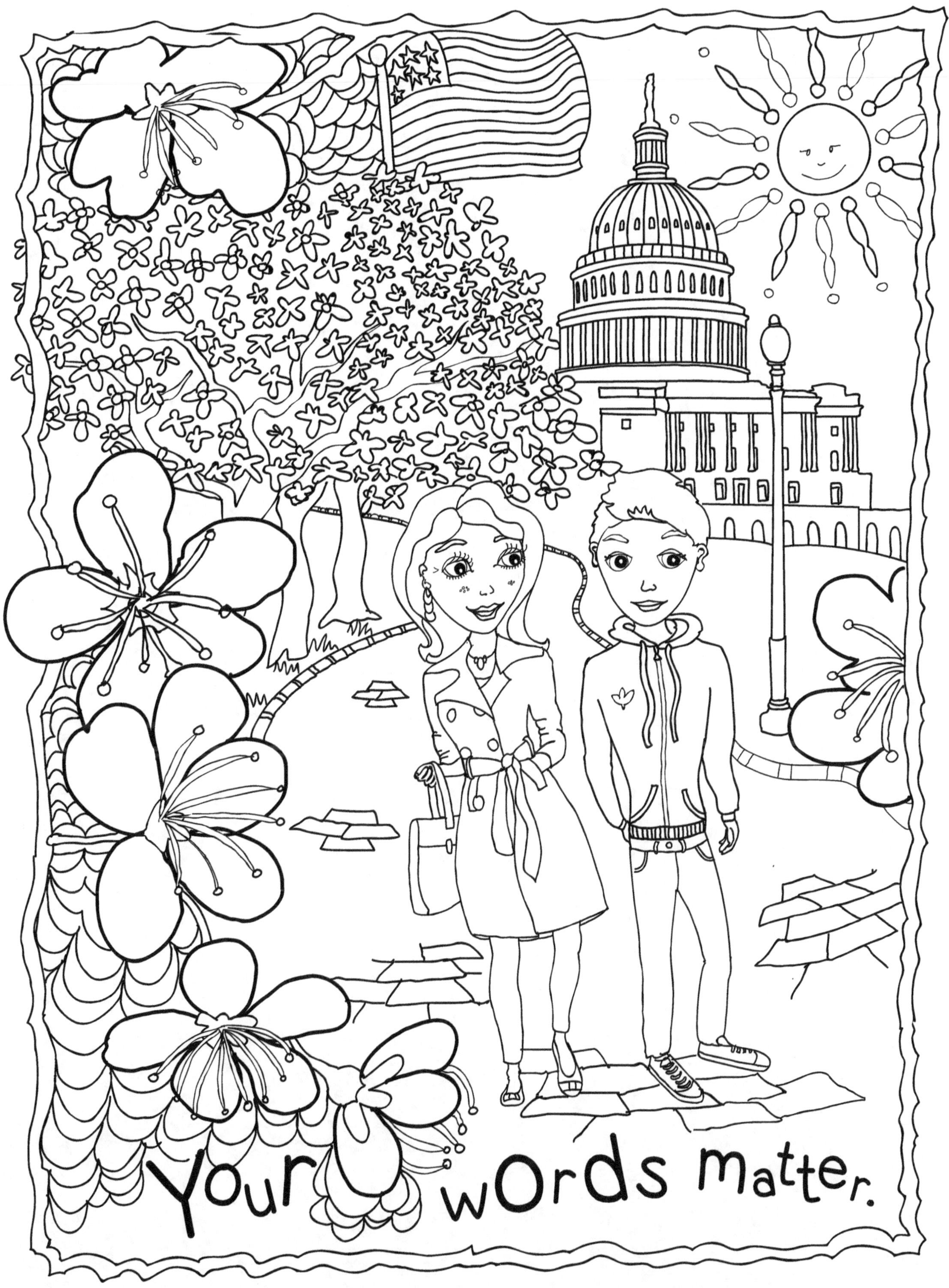

Your wOrds matter.

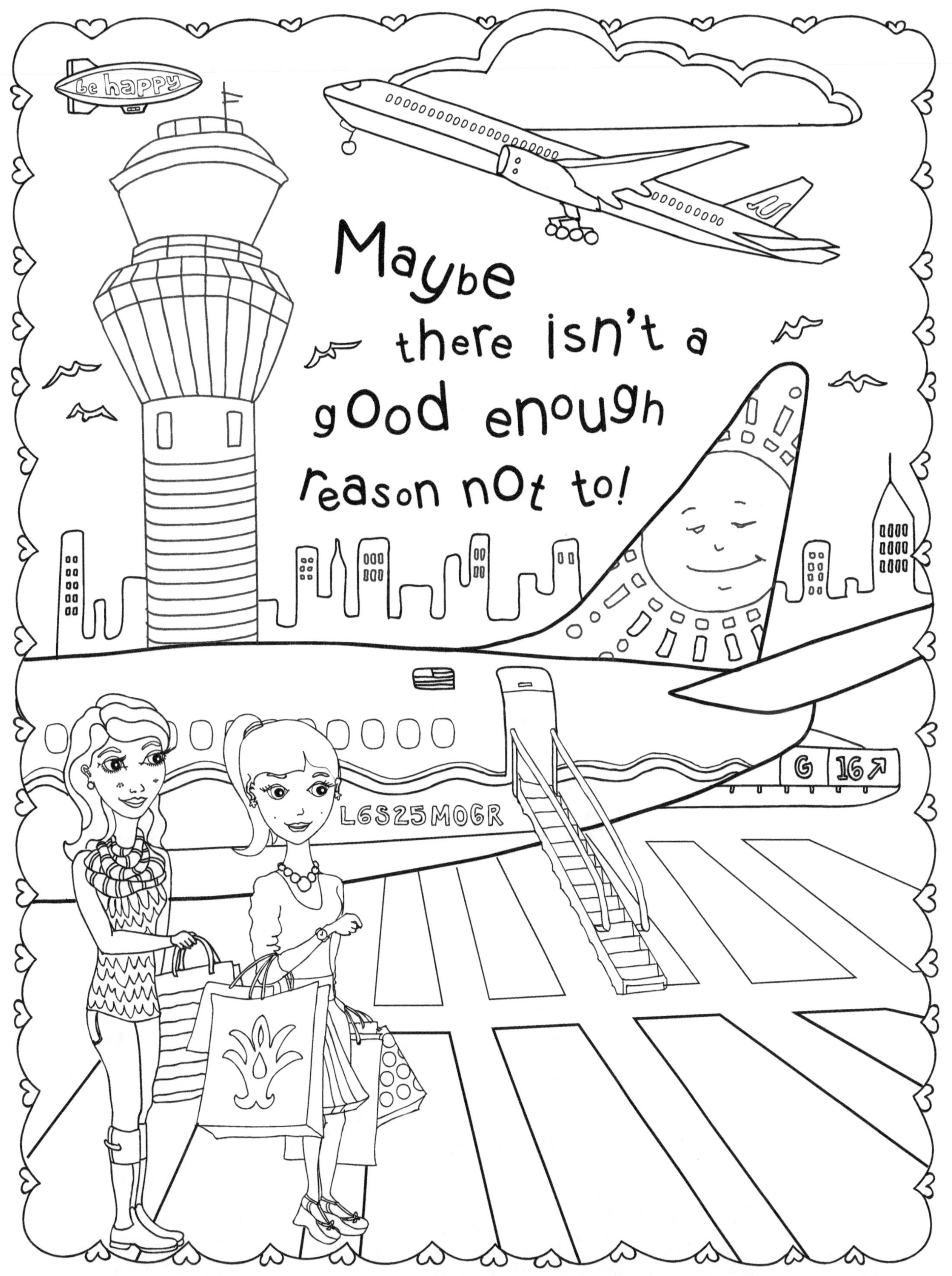

be happy
Maybe there isn't a good enough reason not to!
L6S25MO6R
G 16

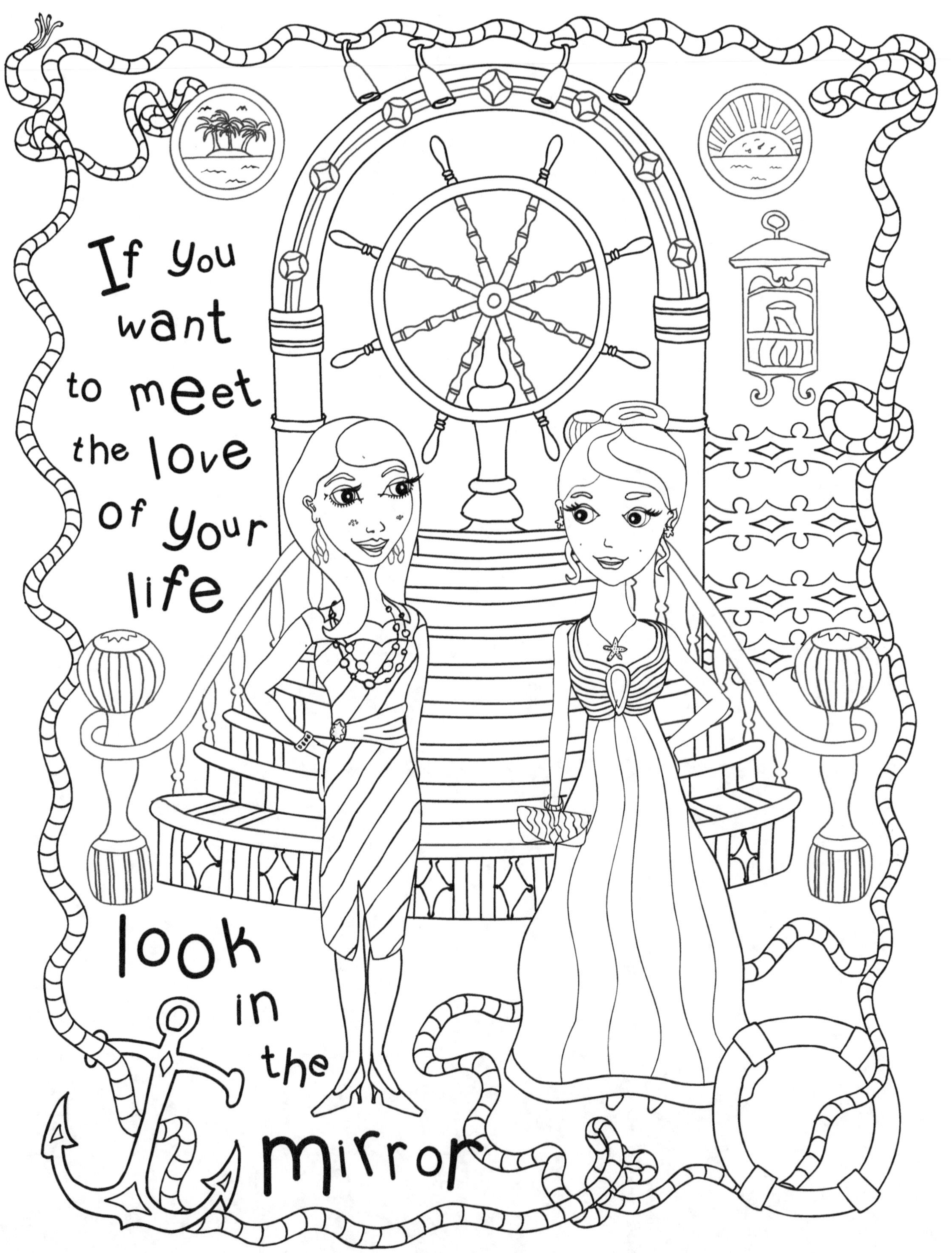

If you want to meet the love of your life
look in the mirror

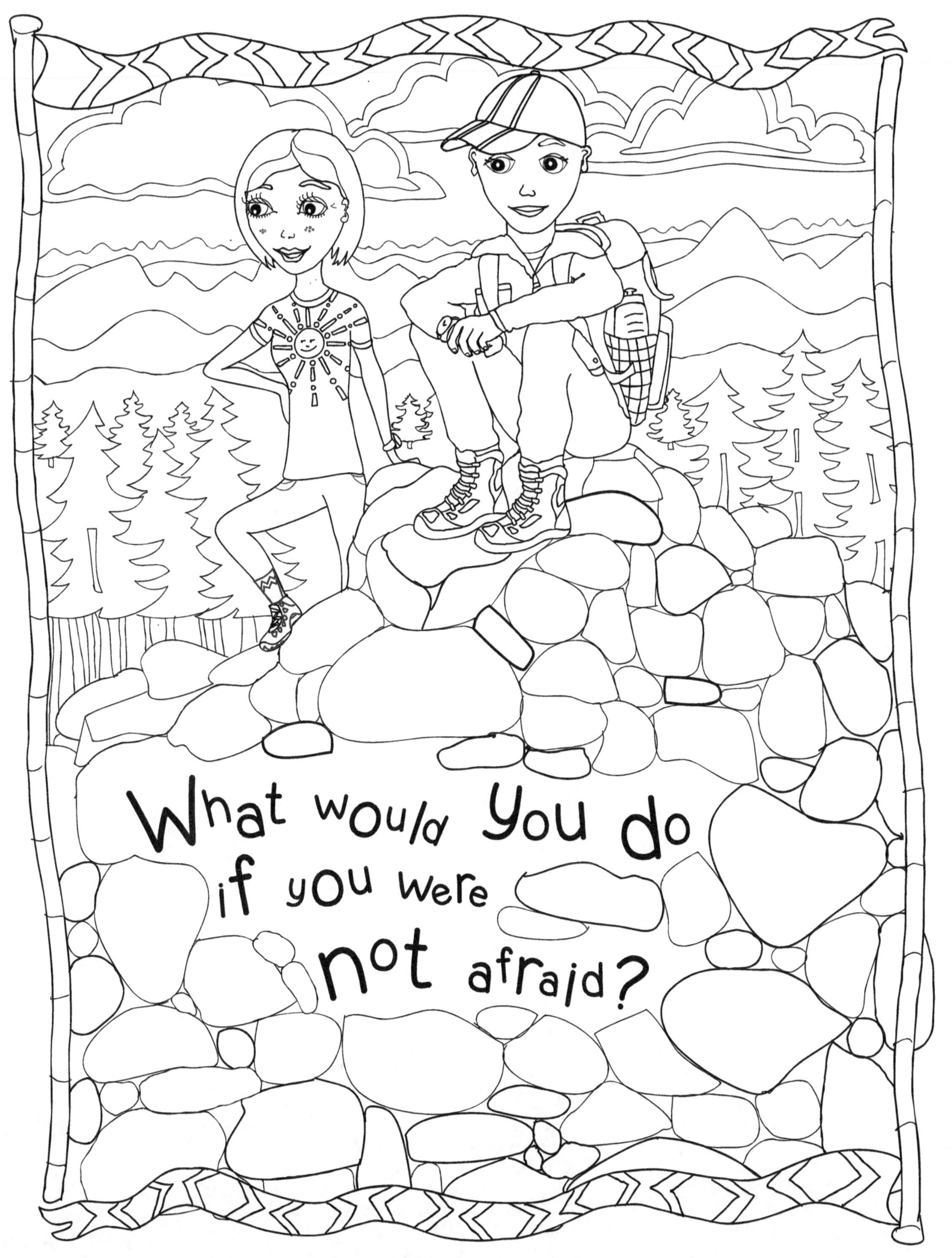

What would you do
if you were
not afraid?

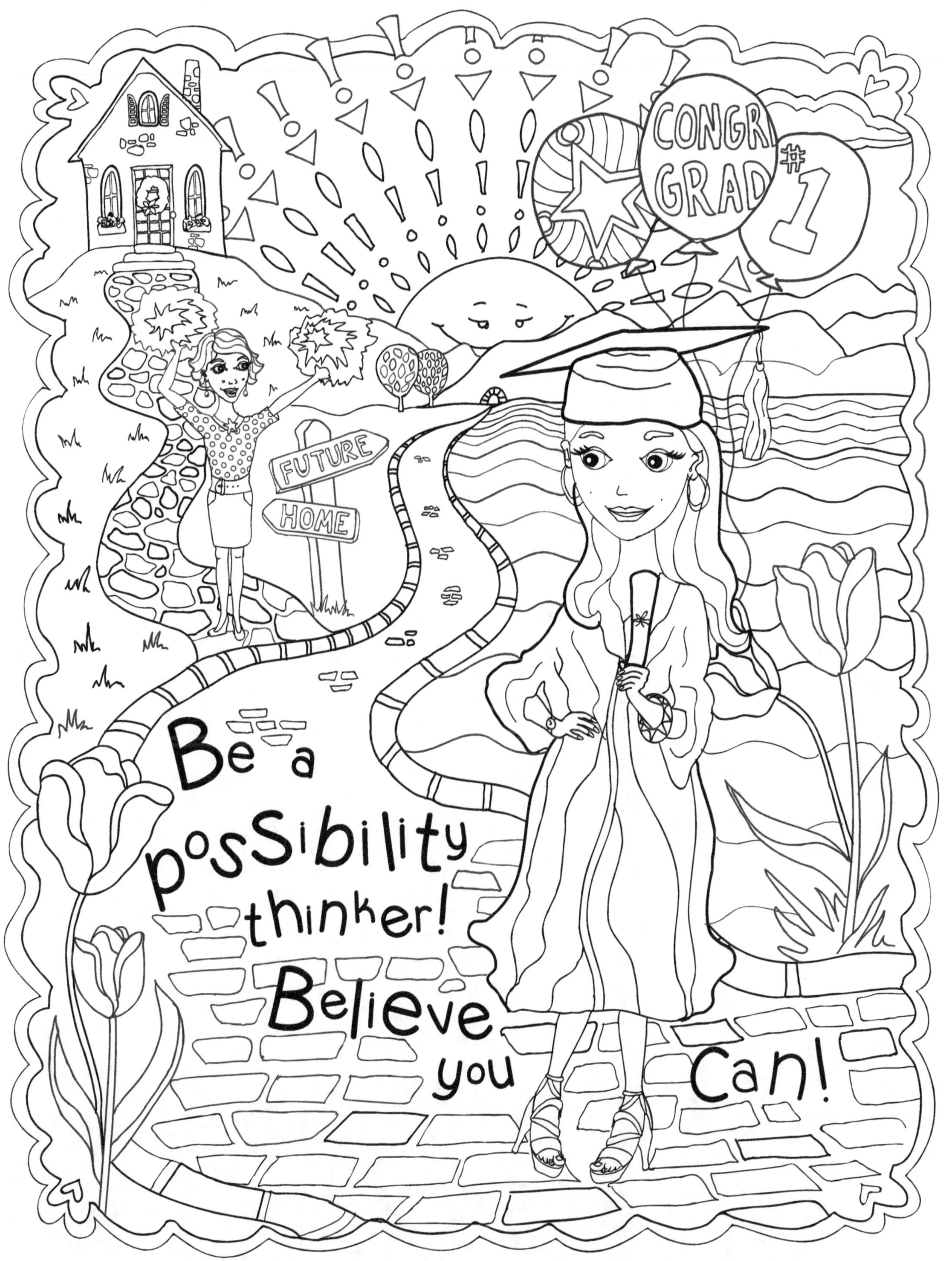

CONGR
GRAD
#1
FUTURE
HOME
Be a
possibility
thinker!
Believe
you
Can!

About the Illustrator

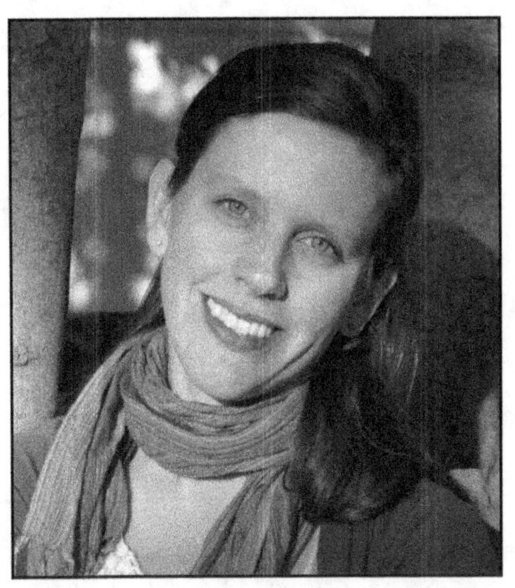

Lesley Vernon is an illustrator, graphic designer and artist. She has illustrated two previous children's coloring books and a number of other book covers, marketing materials and print designs. In addition, Lesley loves sketching and drawing in pen & ink and occasionally dabbles in watercolor too.

Lesley, along with her husband and two young sons, lives in southeastern Massachusetts. She spends her free time hiking and camping in the woods and mountains of New England, exploring the rocky coast of Maine and experimenting with growing vegetables in her garden. She and her family enjoy coloring together, and she hopes Mothers and their children everywhere will love coloring in this book!

To find out more about Lesley's work, please visit her website at:

www.lvdesignhouse.com

About the Author

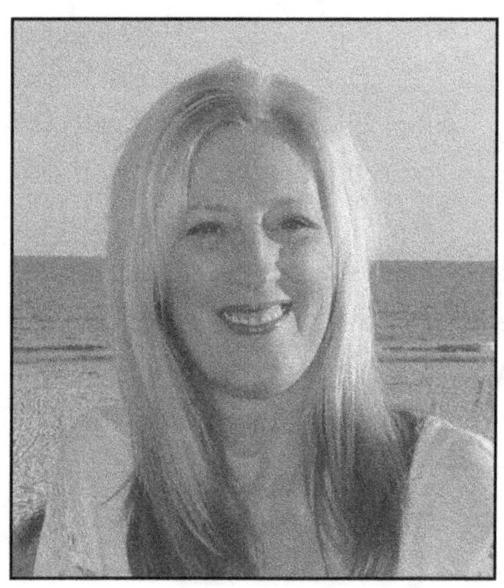

Annette Bridges is an author, publisher and women's retreat host on a mission to help every woman realize her story is extraordinary, valuable and noteworthy.

Before writing books, this former public school and homeschool educator spent a decade writing hundreds of helpful, instructive, and light-hearted columns published by Texas newspapers, parenting magazines, websites and bloggers.

Annette lives on a Texas cattle ranch with her husband John, dachshund Lady and lots of cows. She can drive a tractor but only if wearing a fresh coat of lipstick and it's not her pedicure day!

Annette loves to journal in color and create word art. She especially enjoys coloring with glitter markers. And she looks forward to spending hours with her daughter coloring this book and giggling together as they celebrate many happy adventures.

You can learn more about Annette's books, blogs and videos as well as her women's retreats at:

www.annettebridges.com

Also by Annette Bridges

Oh, how the years fly by!
A whimsical inspirational journey

The Gospel According to Mamma
One mother's philosophy on love, money, God, aging, decisions, change, and much more

Be Queen of Your Life
A savvy mom helps daughters command and rule their lives

Have Lipstick, Will Travel
How to reimagine your life, purpose & hair color

Lady and Bella
Totally Different, Totally Friends

Lady and Bella
Totally friends journal

Lady and Bella's Alphabet Kitchen
A to Z Recipes for Kid Cooks